IWALKᴲꓘAWA

A guide to consciously
igniting your true purpose

By Adam Botha

BALBOA
PRESS

A DIVISION OF HAY HOUSE

Balboa Press books may be ordered through booksellers or by contacting:

Balboa Press
A Division of Hay House
1663 Liberty Drive
Bloomington, IN 47403
www.balboapress.com.au
1-(877) 407-4847

ISBN: 978-1-4525-0836-8 (sc)
ISBN: 978-1-4525-0837-5 (e)

Because of the dynamic nature of the Internet, any web addresses or links contained in this book may have changed since publication and may no longer be valid. The views expressed in this work are solely those of the author and do not necessarily reflect the views of the publisher, and the publisher hereby disclaims any responsibility for them.

The author of this book does not dispense medical advice or prescribe the use of any technique as a form of treatment for physical, emotional, or medical problems without the advice of a physician, either directly or indirectly. The intent of the author is only to offer information of a general nature to help you in your quest for emotional and spiritual well-being. In the event you use any of the information in this book for yourself, which is your constitutional right, the author and the publisher assume no responsibility for your actions.

Any people depicted in stock imagery provided by Thinkstock are models, and such images are being used for illustrative purposes only.

Certain stock imagery © Thinkstock.

Printed in the United States of America

Balboa Press rev. date: 2/16/2013

I dedicate this book to the Divine Infinite, my family and friends, and my ancestors and guides for helping me to awaken to my true purpose.

I am humbled and eternally grateful...

Acknowledgements

My deepest and most heartfelt thanks...

Percy Mosedie, you have always been there for me brother and our journey together continues to higher and greater states of awareness.

Isabel Vidal, for your beautiful transformational and magical work that has had such an impact on my life.

My dearest magical friend *Adele Prins,* your journey of transformation has touched and moved me to no end. Thank you for being part of my incredible transformation.

Antony Tarboton, for your deep transformational work that has awakened me to new levels of understanding of who I am. Thank you.

Lorrine Araujo, for entering my life at such a crucial point. Your amazing love and compassion and support know no end: to our journey deepening and evolving.

Sandy Shoolman, for your selfless gift that has contributed greatly to the end result of this book. Thank you.

Graham De Lacy, for your generosity and wonderful work as a photographer.

To my soul sister *Faiza Garde,* for always being there in love and support.

Dad, for your creative inspiration, passion and lust for life.

Mom, for your unending nurturing love and strength.

My brother *Werner,* for who you are today. Your incredible personal story of transformation inspires me.

My cousin *Mark Butler,* for all of your unconditional support and love.

Nicole Antonie, for your blessing of loving friendship.

Thank you and bless you all with the abundance of living a full life of joy, happiness and love.

CONTENTS

"No heart has ever suffered when it goes in search of its dreams."
- Paulo Coehlo, The Alchemist

PREFACE

Born into a world of sensory overload, we have been distracted.

We have forgotten… Hypnotised by the busy-ness around us, we have been lulled into a deep sleep… a spiritual slumber that's been carrying on for too long.

We have left "who we really are" behind, and traded our true selves to feed the illusion of "who we think" we are. We have settled for less because we were taught that this was the right way – the only way.

But I'm here to share with you "the other way": the way that speaks to your soul and reawakens your spirit, your dreams, and your yearning for a life lived as the highest, most magnificently magical version of yourself!

I'm here to tell you that you don't "have to" anymore. You can allow yourself to let go. You can awaken to what it feels like to be "in-flow": to be alive and free within yourself again.

It's time to reawaken.
It's time to walk awake.

WHERE IT ALL BEGAN
MY PERSONAL STORY

IWALKAWAKE

I chose to emerge into the world as fireworks ignited the sky above Mowbray Maternity Home on the eve of Guy Fawkes Day 1974. Born to an incredibly creative father and courageous loving mother, I was a happy strong baby.

As I grew up, my sensitivity to the energies around me increased immensely. My perception of my surroundings began to mould and shape me as a young child.

As I grew more and more disillusioned by the world around me, I became a child who was extremely introverted. Due to my oversensitivity and concern about what others were doing or thinking of me, I did my own thing. The reality was that the outside world carried on hurting and disappointing me again and again, until I kind of just gave up on it – because what I created with my imagination was far richer and more rewarding than what I was expected to pay attention to.

And the more I imagined, the more I created an inner world where I couldn't be disappointed, because in this world I was writing my script and directing my movie. In this world, I could be anyone or anything I wanted to be: it was a place where magic happened and every moment was filled with enchantment.

You see, I grew up in a household where my parents were divorced – spending the week with my mother and younger brother, and every second weekend at my father's place. It was a tumultuous upbringing being with Mom and missing Dad or vice versa and sometimes incredibly painful not having either of my parents there as Mom was out fighting to earn a living to keep her boys, and Dad was busy working on projects of his own. Deep inside, it disturbed me that my parents weren't together anymore and for years I can remember the glimmer of hope inside of me that maybe, just maybe, there was a chance of them getting back together. Their busy-ness I perceived as unavailability – and left me feeling like I wasn't needed, and that I was unsupported and alone. Not being in control of having my parents there for me, I felt abandoned and vulnerable and, early on in my life, I made the decision to look after me. That was it! I had made my mind up... and was not going to allow anyone to disappoint me ever again.

I remember the first day I had to go to school – it was terrifying. Not only was I being robbed of my time at home, but my safe space – my inner world, my creation – was going to have to take second place in my life. I just knew this in my heart and it devastated me. The very world that I had spent all of my childhood life creating to help me feel safe and secure was about to be compromised in a huge way, and there was nothing I could do to stop it from happening. My eyes were red from crying as I knew what lay ahead. That day, I died to the world I knew.

Going into a world that I did not trust, I felt ultimately betrayed by those who loved me for not allowing me to make a choice: to go or not to go.

In this new world fear was the modus operandi. I was forced to trade a world of imagination, creativity and magic for a world of conformity, emptiness and suffering. I still remember sitting in assembly on Monday mornings and, as we started to sing hymns, a deep sadness would well up within me. The music touched something inside of me that triggered a mourning for the world I had lost. Words cannot describe how sad and lonely I felt on those Monday mornings.

I clung desperately to the time when I could just go home and retreat back into the inner world I knew – the world where I would find the nourishment and love that I needed.

An incredibly creative child with a rich imagination, I would spend hours and hours creating – whether it was building Star Wars or Battle Star Galactica scenes out of Lego, or drawing. This place within which I created was where my spirit thrived. I was only really happy when I was in this space – connected to my imagination and immersed in my creative process.

At school I was very self-conscious: for a long time terrified by this unfamiliar place with other kids with strange habits who seemed not to mind what was going on around them. There was a carefreeness and playfulness that they displayed that I just could not relate to or connect with. I couldn't relate because "carefree" and "playful" only happened inside of me when I was alone, not in the outside world of uncertainty where I felt vulnerable and fearful. While I wanted to "let go" and "just be", I couldn't. My memory of abandonment and distrust was too strong and painful to allow any chance of the experience to repeat itself. In my world, "inside" was safe and "outside" was not.

This was the daunting and exhausting dance that I would carry out for most of my primary school life.

I was often verbally bullied by the kids around me because I was different and never taught how to stand up for myself. To me, conflict meant harming another and all I wanted was a world of peace – a world where I could be nurtured and nurture others. I was taught to feel anxiety and fear in an environment of unpredictability and chaos.

During most of our school holidays, my brother and I would spend time at Gran's with our two cousins who were similar ages to us. The plot of land where my Gran lived was a sanctuary outside of the city surrounded by pine trees that my grandfather planted before he died. These trees stood tall like sentinels protecting my grandmother and family. Gran was the perfect nurturer – she ensured we got all the love, playtime and delicious home cooked food we needed. These were magical times – Gran used to pack little bits and pieces and take us all by the hand, guiding us to a clearing at the edge of the plot where we picnicked and played as the wind whistled through the pine needles. I still remember waking up in Gran's room, to the rooster's crow and Country Morning cereal with warm milk – the crisp fresh farm air filling my nostrils. The love and magic I felt around my Gran gave me momentary hope in the outside world.

At the age of about 13, I slowly began to emerge from my shell and started to learn what it meant to stand up for myself. A childhood friend who would often provoke me was giving me the same trouble as usual – and one day I just had enough. I screamed at him with all the anger I had in me and let him have it. As terrifying as it was for me (because of the amount of anger I discovered was inside of me), I felt really good about standing up for myself.

To eventually say the words "no, that's enough!" often took everything I had. These were words used only when I was pushed to my absolute limit – about to crack – because, at my core, I didn't believe in anger or aggressive behaviour. All I wanted was to feel at peace and in harmony with my environment.

One of my greatest regrets was not giving the girl I had a crush on a drawing I had done of her when she was the still life model in my art class. It really hit home when, a week later, she hooked up with one of my classmates. I beat myself up for weeks after that about not having taken the opportunity to tell her how I felt about her and giving her a gift I thought was really personal.

I learnt that if you don't grab an opportunity the moment it appears, it passes you by and that's it – you can never turn back...

High school was another story. Often I felt very disillusioned with what I was being taught, so I immersed myself in the things I loved – namely art and skateboarding with a close group of friends. When I drew, time stood still. I could carry on for hours and hours without tiring, and the end result was often more than I expected (probably because I didn't expect anything really, I just loved doing it). I loved the focus it gave my mind and found that it immersed me in my imagination where I felt stimulated, nurtured and alive.

Skateboarding was the ideal sport. I could do it alone (which gave me time to practise and perfect my tricks), as well as with my friends (where we learnt from and taught each other what we knew). This was the first time in my life that I felt a genuine sense of belonging to something greater than myself. I felt nurtured and protected by the group, whilst getting to do something I really loved. It was amazing!

It was during this time that I also discovered my love of music. Digging around in my Dad's cupboard one day, I pulled out his old beaten-up 12-string guitar which was strung up as a six-string. The minute my tender fingers hit those rusty strings I knew this was something I would pursue. My friends and I would often jam together, playing our favourite songs – it was a blast every time.

Going out to heavy metal rock venues was another favourite pastime of ours. I absolutely loved heavy metal because it provided me with something I could channel my anger through. Suddenly I was allowed to express it in a safe space where everyone else was doing the same thing. It gave me permission to just "let it all out" which was incredibly liberating for me. Having had a long night out with friends, I felt connected, cleansed and energised by the experience.

After school I went on to study graphic design at college. My love of
alternative music continued and my new group of friends were loyally
aligned to this cause. It was a fun, crazy time spent rocking and creating
and just goofing around most of the time. This carefreeness was exactly
what my spirit needed after all the pressure and workload and exams
during my final year at school. I loved college, not so much for what I was
learning, but rather because of the freshness of the environment and the
new friends I made. Each day was an adventure that became fun and
exciting. Even the bus rides through town were a blast – there was a
bustle of energy down every road we travelled, which gave me time to
plug-in my Walkman, listen to my music and just sit back and watch the
world go by.

I remember the rides putting me in quite a meditative state which relaxed
me and gave me time to reflect on where I was and where I wanted to be.

During my second year of study, one thing led to another and I met the
first true love of my life. I was 19. She was 24, and I felt like the king of my
Universe. Completely in love, every moment crackled with inexhaustible
energy. Colours were brighter. People were more beautiful. Food tasted
better than ever before. I still vividly recall the first night we connected.
She invited me over to a party she was having with a small group of
friends at her place. I arrived and was greeted by this goddess dressed in
black. The first glimpse of her knocked the breath out of me as I struggled
to maintain control over my senses. As our eyes met I just knew this was
going to be insane-amazing. I remember the defining moment during the
course of the evening when we were standing quite close to one another
and she leant her back against mine. I was overcome by a tangible surge
of excitement and energy that rushed through my body – it was like
nothing I had ever experienced before.

After the party had died down, she suggested that the two of us go for a drive to a lookout point on the hillside close by. I was in seventh heaven by the time we got there. The song on the radio was "Drive" by a band called R.E.M. It was one of my favourites and had just become a whole lot more significant by connecting me to this magical adventure.

Never will I ever forget that night. I experienced what falling in love felt like and how out of control it could make me feel. It was terrifying and so damn exciting at the same time!

My first year of work as a junior designer soon arrived. I worked really hard with my full focus and attention on being the best at what I did. It paid off when, after just two years, I was sent to London to receive an award for one of my projects. Sitting on the plane about to take off was incredible – a deep sense of happiness filled me as I reflected on the joy I felt doing this work. I knew this was my time and felt so grateful for the acknowledgement of the award. The stimulation of travel and being in a completely foreign environment blew me away. My senses were on high alert all the time – ready to engage with new people, places and experiences. I felt a great sense of accomplishment which was good for my self-esteem. I learnt that when I do what I love and immerse myself in it, the reward will be greater than the enjoyment of doing it.

A couple of years later I heard about an abundance awareness workshop. I was fascinated by the concept of "abundance" along with the philosophy that there really is enough for everyone on this planet. I knew in my heart that this could only be realised by humanity if we all came back to "balance". I attended this workshop and completely immersed myself in the work. I felt like I had discovered making love for the first time all over again, yet the overwhelming feeling of bliss was far more expanded.

On the workshop I learnt how to meditate properly, and how to cleanse my energy field and tap into the collective field of consciousness. I learnt how to create a "safe haven" within which I could further explore my inner world – a place where I could manifest and imagine my dreams into reality. Being in meditation was an ecstasy that I really battled to describe in words. I would sit for longer and longer periods of time and, the more I sat, the greater the intensity of bliss. I still remember taking my lunch break in the bathroom where I would sit in meditation – it really was the only place in the office where I would not be disturbed! Looking back, I laugh at how I alternated between the upstairs and downstairs bathrooms to try to avoid people thinking I was either crazy or up to some really dodgy stuff. I was meditating three times a day every day. Coming out of meditation eventually became as blissful as being in meditation. I felt a deep sense of connection and love with the Divine. I now saw astounding magical beauty in what before had been ordinary, everyday objects or people. I felt truly touched by the gift of life I had been given.

It became increasingly difficult to work in a corporate nine-to-five job and explore my spirituality. But I carried on working and working and working. The problem was that what I had recently discovered was far more valuable than what I was doing for a living. I almost felt that I was "short-changing" myself by staying in this job which ate up the best part of my day, which I could be spending doing spiritual work.

Looking back, I can honestly say that this was my "fall from grace". This was a time in my life when the Universe was giving me a choice to discover something far greater – an opportunity to engage in my life's work and live my true purpose – and I didn't take that opportunity.

To this day, I can't quite figure out why. Maybe it was fear or my own insecurities. It almost feels like I was distracted. Like I "bought into" what everyone else was saying and living their lives by: get a better house, a better car, a better promotion etc etc – all based on materialism and "ego feeding".

I lost the plot and went off track.

Even though I carried on meditating and studying spirituality and meta-physics, I got more and more lost in the world of materialism. I became more and more concerned about what others thought of me and my image – and that came at a price. My relationships lacked depth and my expenses just kept on growing. The more I got paid, the more I ended up spending, and the more I felt the emptiness inside of me grow.

On the outside I pretended to be okay and fulfilled, yet on the inside I felt a growing desperation and need for true fulfilment. It felt like my "inner" and "outer" worlds were moving further and further apart, and it was affecting me badly. I felt more and more fragmented – as if I was rebelling against my own life.

I realised that no-one else was to blame for where I found myself. My life up until this point had been completely created by me: whether I was conscious of it or not.

It was time to get back on track and move consciously closer to what I was meant to be doing.

One evening, I spoke to a close friend of mine about the idea of going to Sri Lanka on a whim instead of making the same routine trip to the coast to visit my family. He challenged me to do it, and I accepted. Literally two days later I was on a plane to Sri Lanka with a backpack and a Lonely Planet guide, having paid for the whole trip with my credit card. To this day it is one of the most exhilarating things I have ever done.

I felt completely free and as curious as a child. I discovered that true spontaneity takes courage, and that unplanned adventures open up one's intuition like nothing else on earth! It was a trip that showed me the power of my mind and my heart, and my taking immediate action. I realised that if I believed in achieving what I really wanted in life, and seized the opportunities presented to me, I could do anything my heart desired.

I gently ended a relationship that no longer served either of us and began to face my stuff head-on. My intention to consciously uncover the subconscious belief patterns that had been affecting my life was all that mattered to me. I knew I had work to do on myself and I was determined to awaken to the more fulfilling, higher quality existence that I knew in my heart was possible.

I began plunging all my available energy into seeking out why I was the way I was, and began exploring how I could change myself and my life from inside. Through deep self-reflection, life-coaching and process workshops, I can truly say I have awakened to "who I am". I have become more conscious of the old belief patterns that were running me and have awoken to a more conscious, rewarding existence.

I have manifested an incredibly nurturing relationship and rebuilt a loving connection with my family members and friends. I continue on this journey and am stepping into what I like to call "my new life", where I am living what I know is my "true purpose" or destiny.

Yes, there is a part of me that feels apprehensive, yet a bigger part of me knows that now is the time – that this is me walking the dream...
Walking awake.

INTRODUCTION

IWALKAWAKE

WHAT IS ENERGY?

What is energy – really?
Simply put, energy is the connection between all things.

It is the life force that runs through all matter.

Matter is made up of atoms. Atoms are made up of microscopic molecules that spin around a central point. The speed at which these molecules spin is determined by the amount of energy running through them. This "spinning around of molecules" at super high speed creates the illusion of solid matter.

So, if all things are made up of atoms, and the energy running through everything is the same energy, then we are literally connected to everything around us and each other, without even realising it! The dance of this energy takes place on such a subtle and microscopic level that it is invisible to most of us.

Our awakening requires us to realise the above *consciously.*

WHAT IS VIBRATION?

Vibration is the speed at which the molecules spin around an atom.

The reason why matter takes on so many different forms lies in the fact that the atoms (which make up the matter) vibrate at different speeds or frequencies. This difference in vibration determines the characteristics of an object.

The higher the speed of the molecules spinning, the higher the vibration of the object. That's why we say he or she has a good "vibe" about them. People with a good vibe have enabled their energy field to vibrate at a higher level. They have realised their power as magnetic beings who attract what they wish into their lives.

If all matter is in fact energy vibrating at various frequencies, then you have to be made up of this same energy! You are intimately connected to everything and part of all that is. And, if you are part of all that is, and all that surrounds you is a part of you, then you have the power to affect all that is within and all that which surrounds you.

You are the magician of your own reality...

Your thoughts, feelings and actions are all forms of energy that contribute to your reality.

They are creating your life as we speak right now.

WHO ARE WE?

We are all Source Energy.

This energy is not something that lies outside of ourselves. It is us and we are it! There really is no separation. We are the micro and the macrocosm.

Within each of us lies the entire Universe. We are limitless, infinite beings having an experience in a human body.

This is really who we are.

WHY SHOULD WE RAISE OUR VIBRATION?

We have lost our connection of living in harmony with nature, and most of us spend far too much time in artificial environments where the energy is stagnant and creates negatively-charged particles called "negative ions".

These particles attach themselves to our auric field and literally weigh heavily on our energy fields or "pull us down".

Think of how a magnet attracts iron filings – eventually you can't even see the magnet beneath the heavy layer of grey. This is what our energy bodies often look like. So how do we combat this to keep our energy strong and positively-charged?

We raise our vibration!

As already explained, when we raise our vibration, we create positive change within. The effect of this is positive change outside of ourselves. When we raise the vibration of our energy body, we literally open the door to a better and more fulfilling existence.

Over-pollution and the stress in our cities create negative ions. These are negatively-charged particles that cling to our magnetic energy field and reduce the frequency at which our energy bodies vibrate. We need to combat this by raising our vibration.

Raising our vibration makes it far more difficult for these negative ions to attach themselves to our energy fields. This is because "like attracts like" – if we are vibrating at a higher level we will automatically attract positive energy into our lives. In this way we Awaken Harmony. By resonating positively, we attract positivity – simple!

WHAT ARE THE NINE AWAKENINGS?

The *Nine Awakenings* are principles designed to assist you to live the life of your highest potential:

A life of connection to all that is around you and within you; a life of feeling and expressing who you are; a life without fear – where anything is possible...

Awaken AWARENESS "I am"
You are Creation and Creator. Enjoy practising bringing things into being. You are both the magic and the magician. Exercise your power as a creative being. *It's your life!*

Awaken CONNECTION "I ignite"
You are infinitely connected to everything around you. It is you and you are it. Take time out to remember and feel the magical connection you have with the entire Universe.

Awaken HARMONY "I flow"
Flow with and not against yourself, and notice how your external world falls into place. Effortlessly, all things flow to you and around you. You are in the stream of *harmonious connection* with all that is! Let go of the struggle and go with the flow: *go to where you feel alive!*

Awaken CONCENTRATION "I desire"
Where your concentration goes, your energy flows. You receive what you focus on. Concentrate your thoughts, feelings and actions on achieving your highest potential. Focus on that which you wish for. You are the genie of your own life. *Your wish is granted...*

Awaken *FORGIVENESS "I love"*
Allow yourself to forgive yourself and others. Let go of all your hate, anger and pain. Activate the flow of love into your life. Open your heart and discover so much more.

Awaken *RESPONSIBILITY "I choose"*
Every thought, feeling and action *you create* has an effect. Your life up until now is completely of your own making. *Accept this* and you will take the first step in creating your future.

Awaken *GRATITUDE "I feel'*
Become grateful for what you *do have* – right here and right now. The *Universe appreciates being appreciated,* and will reward your gratitude. Say *"thank you"* more often, from the heart.

Awaken *SURRENDER "I trust"*
Surrender to your highest potential. Surrender yourself to what you really want in your life. Get out of your own way and all external obstacles will remove themselves. Detach from the outcome and trust in the Universal intelligence that's at work for you: it knows exactly what you want!

Awaken *PURPOSE "I belong"*
You are a crucial part of the whole – you bring with you an exquisitely original energy to the world. *It is now up to you to explore, discover and live your life's purpose!* Thank yourself for being you.

The following pages will go into further detail regarding the Nine Awakenings, and will provide practical exercises to assist you in discovering your highest potential and true purpose.

THE NINE AWAKENINGS
IGNITING YOUR TRUE PURPOSE

AWAKEN AWARENESS "I am"

YOU ARE CREATION AND CREATOR.

Focusing your mind on being fully aware of your thoughts is the first step to understanding your power as a creative being. What are you thinking? Become aware of your body: your feelings. What are you feeling? Become aware of your actions. What are you doing? Expand your awareness. Remain conscious.

Who I am

Keeping "who I am" separate from "what I do" requires detachment. I step into different roles at different times:
- being "the son" when I'm with my parents;
- being "the designer" when I'm at work;
- being "the guide" when I'm with friends;
- being "the romantic" when I'm with my lover.

I find a multiple array of personas playing this "game of life". However, beneath all of these personas that I like to attach myself to, that I allow myself to identify with, exists an ever-present consciousness that is aware that it is observing my "game of life".

We were all born into a physical body with a family and a set of life circumstances that we chose and agreed to experience before we came here. Every experience we knew we would need, we chose before we entered our physical form. This is the "game of life" that we agreed to play a role in before entering into this physical realm.

Who was I before I came here? I was original soul energy – an integral part of the All-Knowing One. And this is who I am right now. You see, soul energy (or all energy for that matter) cannot be destroyed or created: it has and always will be in existence. So you could say that we are really soul energy visiting here in a physical body. We are "just visiting", soon to move on to other realms of light and love. This life is not a destination. It is a visitation – it is transitory, just like all things in this Universe. For example, you don't go on vacation and think to yourself: "This is it." You go to enjoy the experience of allowing, of letting go, of getting back in touch with yourself (or that which makes you happy).

Have you ever thought about where the words "vacation" or "holiday" come from? Well, one comes from the word "vacate" meaning "to leave" where we were before. The other comes from the word "holy" alluding to that which is sacred and special to us. Why is it then that we have to "leave" our current situation or life to reach that which is sacred or Divine? Why can't we find that which is sacred and special to us, and do it every day of our lives? This is the question we should be asking ourselves. In finding the answer, we would never have to take another day's "leave" in our lives – every moment would be "sacred" and "special" to us.

Getting back "in touch" with that which feeds our souls is why we are here. The Divine wants us to celebrate and enjoy every single moment here! "So why don't we?" you ask. Well, because we have been trained to conform to be something that "we are not". And this something that

"we are not" is being experienced by us to remind us of "who we are".
We have been taught to fill our path with "obstacles", so that we believe
that "struggle" is part of life. It wouldn't be if we just let go and trusted!

Because the Universal flow of this energy force is akin to the flow of water
(and you don't see water flowing up a mountain side do you?), it springs
from its source and flows in the direction of least resistance to eventually
return to its source – just like we do as souls on a journey returning to our
Source.

How much happier would you feel if you just let go? If you stopped
clinging desperately out of fear? If you released yourself from the daily
struggle within? Can you imagine the freedom your soul would feel?
How much more energy you would have to do what you really love, to
be who you always wanted to be, to make a difference in the world that
excited you every time you thought about it?

The art of letting go and discovering that which moves you within is
an invaluable tool in navigating your reconnection back to Source.
Am I being true to who I am? My light, my dark? Who am I now? Yes,
I can point fingers and look "outside" to define who I am. I can be the
judge. However, if I choose to judge outside of myself, I must judge that
which is inside myself (which is in and of itself the same thing). The outer
world mirrors the inner world. The outer illusion is the result of our inner
creation – isn't that just beautiful? The imagery being projected on your
screen is yours to direct – is yours to create! So create with a focused
mind and a conscious heart!

Rather than resent or judge others or yourself, choose to see this reality
of light and dark within you as the whole of who you are (a complete
human being) with an infinite range of experiences to choose from.

You are free to choose your experiences as you wish. Your experiences don't depend on outer circumstances but rather on the lens you choose to see or feel them through. Which lens are you choosing? Choose consciously because it is shaping your perception which, in turn, is determining your experience, and your life in present time.

We can learn how to release ourselves from being judged and judging others. We can say to ourselves: "I choose to be free of judgement and criticism. I release it and embrace the whole spectrum of life as human nature – all of us nurturing what we need to in some way or another."

Embrace yourself. Embrace the whole of yourself. Take a moment to feel the infinite choices right at your fingertips. These moments are yours to mould, bend and sculpt in any which way you wish to: a massive blank canvas just waiting, just beckoning to be nurtured and adorned with your genius. You are the master. You are the chosen one. Embrace your genius. Awaken your awareness...

Check in with yourself: am I aware of my thoughts? What am I thinking right now? Do I wish to continue thinking this thought? Is it serving me or not? Observe your thoughts carefully – they are creating your world. Ask yourself: how am I feeling? And why? Did I choose these feelings? Start becoming conscious of your feelings.

Write down your answers and pay attention to what has just been revealed from within you. All the answers you need are inside of you.

PRACTICES IN AWAKENING AWARENESS

If you want to explore how to awaken your awareness then read on for practices aligned to assist you in doing this.

Probably the most important thing you can use to enhance the quality of how you live is the power of routine. When you repeat an exercise or new habit 28 times, it becomes a part of you. This is because the amount of energy invested decreases dramatically allowing you to complete the routine without thinking about it. You allow it to become part of you thereby creating newer, better patterns that collectively enhance your life. One of the routines I would recommend you develop to enhance your process of awakening is that of meditation.

The only way to let the spirit within you speak is to still your mind. The only way to still your mind is through meditation. Meditation holds the key to accessing the power within you. Being able to still your mind is the first step towards becoming more conscious of who you are and awakening your awareness.

Meditation 01: awaken AWARENESS within you

Find a quiet space where you won't be disturbed.

Sit with your spine upright and breathe consciously. Take three deep breaths. Breathe in deeply, hold each breath a while and then let it out through slightly pursed lips. Each time you breathe out, feel your body and mind relax completely.

After completing this breathing cycle, take your time to slowly become aware of the sounds in the room. Then, gently expand your awareness to include the sounds just outside the room. As you continue to listen, allow yourself to get lost in the detail and layers of the various qualities and nuances of the sounds being presented to you. Let go and become one with the sounds around you. Relax deeply and enjoy the presence of life and energy surrounding you. Once you feel ready (10 –15 minutes should suffice), gently bring yourself out of meditation. Say silently to yourself, "Wide awake. I am wide awake." This meditation is best when done first thing in the morning or last thing at night.

By expanding your awareness in this way, you will cause your auric field to expand. Too often we keep our energy contracted and small due to fear and the chaos going on around us in our busy lives. This meditation will allow you to let go and rejuvenate yourself by expanding your awareness.

Visualisation 01: awaken AWARENESS within your energy field

Sit upright in a chair with your back supported or in the lotus position with your spine straight and your hands on your knees. Take three deep breaths. With each exhalation, feel your body and mind relax from the top of your head to the tips of your toes. When you feel completely relaxed begin your visualisation.

Start by imagining a bright ball of red energy at the base of your spine. Breathe into it, gently sending love to this part of your energy body. See it intensify, expand and grow – all the while feeling a deep sense of safety and security within you. Gently release your attention from this area...

Shift your attention to where your navel is and imagine a bright ball of orange energy in this area. See it, feel it and breathe into it – gently sending love to this part of your energy body. Feel this part of your energy grow and expand with each breath, increasing your desire for fulfilment and joy. Gently release your attention from this area...

Move your loving attention to your solar plexus area, imagining a bright ball of yellow energy here. Breathe into it. Love it. Feel it pulsating and expanding with each breath you take, increasing your sense of inner power and strength. When you are ready, gently release your attention from this area..

Bring your attention up to your heart energy centre (in your chest) and imagine a bright ball of fresh green energy. Breathe into it with love and compassion. Each breath you take expands and grows this loving centre. Feel the love radiate within you.

Gently shift your attention to the base of your throat and imagine a bright ball of blue energy in this area of your body. Feeling your connection, breathe into it – expanding it with each breath. See it. Feel this pulsating beautiful vibrant blue light getting stronger. Intensify this feeling and then gently release your attention from this part of your energy body...

Now move your attention upwards to the point between your eyes at the base of your forehead. Imagine a ball of radiant purple energy here. Feel love and nurturing energy flowing into this space with each breath you take. See the energy expanding and growing. Imagine your intuition increasing from this area. Gently release your attention from this part of your body...

Next focus your awareness on the area just above the crown of your head. Imagine a ball of bright violet energy here. Breathe into it. Feel your awareness of spirit grow and expand as you breathe. Allow its brightness to intensify – and then gently release your attention from this part of your energy body...

Finally focus on the space about half a metre above your head. Imagine a bright white ball of light energy here. Breathe loving intention into it, feeling it grow and expand, and become even brighter with each breath. Allow this sensation to intensify until the white light from this energy centre overflows like a fountain down into your other energy centres. Feel the light cascade and flow and fill your entire auric field. Allow it to fill your whole body. Now infuse the light surrounding you with sparkles of pure golden sunlight flowing in from the top of your head. Relax as your entire energy body pulsates with this life-giving golden white sparkling energy.

Breathe love into your energy body until you feel it expand and grow to about half a metre around you. Feel the energy you have created move and flow within this space. This is your space. You are safe and protected within this space.

Once you feel ready (10 –15 minutes should suffice), gently bring yourself out of meditation. Say silently to yourself, "Wide awake. I am wide awake."

Done once a day in the evening, this visualisation will realign and rejuvenate all of your energy centres.

This visualisation will expand you, grow you and intentionally connect you with your Divine Source. It will make you feel completely balanced and restore you to your natural radiant self.

Exercise 01: awaken AWARENESS in nature

Take a walk in nature. Find a park or large body of water where you can walk around breathing deeply. The air around wide open spaces flows freely and is charged with high quality, life-giving energy. This will purify and energise you as you breathe it in. Walk for 20 – 30 minutes a day. Whilst doing this just let go, expand your awareness and feel your connection to Mother Nature's celebration of being alive – feel your connection to every plant, every flower and every creature, and know that you are part of her beautiful celebration as Creation.

Affirmation 01: affirming AWARENESS

Create your own set of unique affirmations that will assist you. Start with the words "I am..." Always affirm using positive language – never negative language. When you read, recite or chant your affirmation, feel it in your heart. Get in touch with what you are telling yourself. Keep it authentic. Believe it.

Some examples to assist in awakening your AWARENESS are:

I AM
I AM AWARENESS
I AM CREATOR
I AM WITHIN
I AM WHOLE
I AM ENOUGH AS I AM

Remember that your feelings activate the power within the affirmation you have created. Your feelings bring the magic into the affirmation. Always say your affirmations with love and joy.

SET YOURSELF FREE

Peel back the layers
Let go of the façade

It serves you no longer
Be who you are

Let it go
I know it hurts

Yet beneath all that you have clung to
Resides the jewel of You

The light your soul seeks is calling
Saying "shine on me"

In every waking moment
It yearns to set you free

Let it
Set you free

- ADAM BOTHA

AWAKEN CONNECTION "I ignite"

YOU ARE INFINITELY CONNECTED TO EVERYTHING AROUND YOU.

Your infinite connection means that you are everything and everything is you – there is truly no separation. That which surrounds you
affects you and, in turn, you affect it. You affect it by the way in
which you interact with it, so choose wisely. Choose for the better-
ment of yourself and the world around you. Control your choices
consciously – and awaken this connection.

Become the Master of your Universe!

As within, so without

You might think you know and understand completely who you are. Yes,
you have a name. Yes, you have a personality. Yes, you have a job title.
However, I am here to tell you that you are so much more! You are so
much more than these labels and attachments.

You are a being who is intimately connected to *all that is* and *all that
ever will be.* Don't believe this because I tell you it is so. Rather reach into
yourself – close your eyes and *feel the connection for yourself.* Feel this
connection you have with all life – this intimate infinite connection.

Who you are is truly magnificent and in need of celebration – the ultimate
celebration. Awaken this connection and start to love and honour yourself
– know that you are Divine Energy that is manifest. Feel the Divine love as
you read this. Remind yourself of this. And know in your heart that it is true.

Look around you to see this truth: truth that all that is without (outside of yourself) is a reflection of that which is within you. Look within and you will understand all that surrounds you. *Change your within and you will change your without.* Just by changing the way you think and feel (that which is inside of you), you will change the world outside of you. Isn't this reason enough to celebrate? Isn't this connection magnificent?

Your awakening comes at such a crucial time for the world. You are being called to honour the whole of your being – *to bless the whole of your being.*

Know that you are a sacred creative force. You are being invited to step up your game, to stop pursuing your subconscious addictions to pain or pleasure, and to leave your cocoon and fly. It is time to allow your transformation as a connected being to carry you to a higher, lighter, more fulfilled existence.

Let go of all that you've been recycling for so long, and choose a more enlightened, compassionate, graceful, real way of being. Recognise that you are a one-of-a-kind miracle of nature – made to perfection. Stop questioning and feeling that you are less than/not good enough. Stop delaying your greatness. It's time to shine.

So many of us play the waiting game – waiting for something to call us to our purpose. We look for outside signs to direct us to our inner truth. Looking outside for the clarity and truth of purpose that is already inside each one of us is a futile exercise. These answers can only be found inside.

It takes courage to lead your soul to where it feels alive: to where you want to use each day to really live and make a difference; to leave a legacy and the world in a better state. Take heart though, there are many of us who have started walking this path, who feel this yearning to break out of our programmed prison and are ready to open up to the Universal energy. There are many souls questioning how to meet their bliss and walk in the dream here on earth. I am on this journey with you. I know what you are feeling because I feel it myself – right here, right now.

The energy of Awakening is touching more and more of us each day, yearning to elevate our consciousness to give and receive more love. We are being called to shed the shackles of the insatiable appetite of the ego and just be grateful and happy for what we have, including the small things that we take for granted; our healthy bodies with six senses, our loved ones and those who love us.

You see, you're not like everyone else. All of us are individuals yet part of the greater collective – a Divine dichotomy that plays itself out throughout our entire lives. Each of us is required to embrace our uniqueness and discover the role we need to play in the bigger picture. These two aspects of our lives are intricately connected to each other. First we need to discover who we are and what makes us unique. Then we need to go out into the world to share this gift of discovery with others. This is the gift that we bring to the world. It is us: we are that gift. We are the gift we have been waiting for.

In awakening your connectedness, you will start asking yourself how and where you feel your soul click in; where you can make your maximum impact felt and how you can touch as many lives around you as possible. You might also ask how you can make yourself heard and how you can leave a heartfelt impression on the world around you.

Know that you are purposefully connected to the whole; you can empower this connection by doing the work you need to. Start by allowing and getting in touch with the infinite energy within you! This is the most powerfully transformational beautiful work you will ever be a part of: it will be the work of your life. Your life... Because within the life you have lived up to now is contained an infinite number of experiences on so many levels: unique experiences that the person next to you is now connected with in a different way. Perhaps their perceptions and way in which they allowed the experience to impact them were similar to yours, but they would not have been the same.

So you see, you are a wealth of experience waiting to transfer itself and its learnings into a much bigger pool than yourself. You are a part of experience that yearns to transmit itself into the world at the highest level: to be shared and loved and contribute to the world. You are a very necessary, very valuable part of the whole – a part (not "apart") of everything you desire to be connected to and shared with and recognised by.

Together we can transcend into a super state of awareness and celebrate our lives... All one, all connected.

Embrace your connection to everyone and everything. Take a moment to feel the infinite connection right at your fingertips. This connection is yours to explore and celebrate. You are the master. You are the chosen one. Embrace your genius. Awaken your connection...

Check in with yourself: do I feel connected to my world? Am I aware of how I am affecting that which surrounds me? Am I happy with the results of how I am affecting my surroundings? Am I happy with how my surroundings are affecting me? Do I show compassion for others and Mother Earth? Feel your connection consciously.

Write down your answers and pay attention to what has just been revealed from within you. All the answers you need are inside of you.

PRACTICES IN AWAKENING CONNECTION

If you want to explore how to awaken your connection then read on for practices aligned to assist you in doing this.

Probably the most important thing you can use to enhance the quality of how you live is the power of routine. When you repeat an exercise or new habit 28 times, it becomes a part of you. This is because the amount of energy invested decreases dramatically allowing you to complete the routine without thinking about it. You allow it to become part of you thereby creating newer, better patterns that collectively enhance your life. One of the routines I would recommend you develop to enhance your process of awakening is that of meditation.

The only way to let the spirit within you speak is to still your mind. The only way to still your mind is through meditation. Meditation holds the key to accessing the power within you. Being able to still your mind is the first step towards becoming more conscious of who you are and awakening your connection.

Meditation 02: awaken CONNECTION

Find a quiet space where you won't be disturbed.

Sit with your spine upright and breathe consciously. Take three deep breaths. Breathe in deeply, hold each breath a while and then let it out through slightly pursed lips. Each time you breathe out, feel your body and mind relax completely.

After completing this breathing cycle, become aware of where your mind is going – just observe your thoughts. Allow your breath to gain its own rhythm and let go of your focus on your breath. (Each breath will become lighter and lighter until it becomes so light that it seems as though you're not breathing.) Continue to deepen your relaxation whilst expanding your awareness within. Your mind will wander. Be the observer and gently bring it back to your centre. As you deepen your meditation, there will be moments when you stop being aware that you're meditating. These moments of stillness are the moments when you are merging with Source Energy. Allow these moments of emptiness to rejuvenate you.

Once you feel ready (10 – 15 minutes should suffice), gently bring yourself out of meditation. Say silently to yourself, "Wide awake. I am wide awake."

By allowing your connection in this way, you will cause your auric field to expand. Too often we keep our energy contracted and small due to fear and the chaos going on around us in our busy lives. This meditation will enable you to let go and rejuvenate yourself by allowing your connection. It can be done at any time of the day to lift your energy level.

Visualisation 02: awaken CONNECTION within your energy field

Sit upright in a chair with your back supported or in the lotus position with your spine straight and your hands on your knees. Take three deep breaths. With each exhalation, feel your body and mind relax from the top of your head to the tips of your toes. When you feel completely relaxed begin your visualisation.

Say silently to the space around and within you: "Wherever I go, I now vibrate positive loving energy into the world. My energy transforms any negative energy into positive life-giving energy for all those whose lives I touch." See and feel ripples of golden white life-giving energy flowing out of your heart centre into the world. Feel it, and know that the love you are sending out is affecting and healing the world around you. By merely holding the intention and energy of love, you are affecting the world around you by increasing the vibration of love. Your individual intention has affected the whole of humanity. You are the blessing and the blessed. Be still for a moment and honour yourself and the miracle of creation around you.

Once you feel ready (10 – 15 minutes should suffice), gently bring yourself out of meditation. Say silently to yourself, "Wide awake. I am wide awake."

Know that this visualisation will expand you, grow you and intentionally connect you with your Divine Source. You will feel completely balanced and restored to your natural radiant self.

Done once a day first thing in the morning, this visualisation will activate your positive power as a being of love.

Exercise 02: awaken CONNECTION in nature

Try to spend five to 10 minutes a day with your shoes off standing on the grass so that your feet can reconnect with the earth. Stand still and breathe in and out deeply. Feel yourself "rooted": feel your reconnection with Mother Earth as you draw power and energy into your body through the soles of your bare feet. Feel alive!

This exercise is a means of combating our disconnection from the earth. We spend most of our days disconnected. Rubber soles "insulate" us – preventing us from receiving natural energy from the earth. Tarred roads and our cars' rubber tyres further disconnect us from being naturally energised. Have you ever watched children play barefoot outdoors? They seem to play without tiring. This is because their auric fields are being constantly recharged by the earth's energy. Their two feet create a circuit of energised current with Mother Earth allowing their natural flow and balancing energy to be maintained.

The best time to do this exercise is first thing in the morning while there's still dew on the grass outside. Dew that has collected overnight is charged with energy of a high vibration which will be absorbed through your feet, leaving you feeling refreshed and energised throughout the day.

Affirmation 02: affirming CONNECTION

Create your own set of unique affirmations that will assist you. Start with the words "I am..." Always affirm using positive language – never negative language. When you read, recite or chant your affirmation, feel it in your heart. Get in touch with what you are telling yourself. Keep it authentic. Believe it.

Some examples to assist in awakening your CONNECTION are:

I IGNITE
I AM CONNECTED
I AM CONNECTED TO THE DIVINE
I AM ABUNDANT
I AM LOVE
I AM LOVED

Remember that your feelings activate the power within the affirmation you have created. Your feelings bring the magic into the affirmation. Always say your affirmations with love and joy.

NEW LIFE

New found inspiration
New blood
Newfound friends
New family

New me

Loving
Living
Centring
Inspiring
Daring

New me

Self expression
Guilt free
Angerless
Fearless
All loving

New me

- ADAM BOTHA

AWAKEN HARMONY "I flow"

REALISE YOUR HARMONIOUS RELATIONSHIP WITH ALL THAT IS.

Let go of the struggle. Let go of the dis-ease you feel (the worry, the fear and anxiety). Let go of them now. Try to be "in the now" more often (not dwelling in the past or the imagined future), and enter into the flow and harmony of Universal Energy that moves effortlessly through you.

Appreciate this moment here and now. The experience you are having right now is all that is real. The rest is an illusion. (The time and energy you expend on your past and your future will be freed up if you live more consciously in the present by really appreciating every moment of your life as it arrives.)

Become a witness to the miracle of your life and how you can affect everything around you with your energy. Try to notice the magic in the small things. Feel at ease with the Universal Energy – it knows your innermost desires and will assist you if you trust it.

The treasure within

Listen to the conversations around you. So many of us wish away the present – living in "if only": "If only I were on holiday…" or "If only I could have more free time, more money, a better car or house…" The question then becomes: will that really bring you greater happiness? Maybe momentarily. However, after a short while, the hole that you were trying to fill with all these things will once again open with the awareness of your reality. Then you will find yourself back where you started, desiring the next "best thing" in a bid to make you feel worthy and better about yourself.

You see, we have been taught to measure our true happiness and worth in terms of the physical stuff that we own (or that owns us depending on which way you look at it). This "stuff" is unfortunately not the answer to our ultimate dreams of happiness, harmony and real fulfilment.

If I were to ask you what would excite you beyond measure, what would your answer be? If you could, what would you be doing that would delight you as you rise to greet each new day – where your work didn't feel like work anymore because of how much you loved what you were doing; because of how great you felt doing it? Imagine if making a life and making a living felt as natural as the rays of sunshine greeting you every morning.

What I'm talking about is your purpose: the real reason why you and I are here on earth now... The thing that makes your soul sing – that moves you to get up every day with joy in your heart; the thing that moves you to a place of connection and harmony with yourself and others.

Your purpose helps you feel that you belong. It helps you give of yourself not because you feel you have to, but because there is nothing else you would rather spend your time doing. It fills you with a burning desire to share yourself with the world you live in. Your purpose constantly encourages you to work towards making a difference in the world, – knowing in your heart that you're doing your best and will leave the world a better place than you found it.

How do we awaken to why we're here? How do we discover and commit to this purpose? How do we soothe our soul's yearning? By listening. By really listening to that hunch, that gut feeling, that gentle voice within, that light tug deep inside that whispers, "Let go. I will show you."

You see, when we stop doing things the same way we've always done them, magic happens! We have to consciously do this though.

We need to let go and awaken to the "reality" that we are creating the illusion around us – from deep within ourselves. Because our unique set of circumstances and beliefs have created our perceptions, and our perceptions are creating our "reality" (the illusion that many of us are not aware of), we are constantly creating our own "world" which we view and experience through our own set of lenses. This means that our "reality" is completely under our control and has been from the word "go!"

That's right: you and I are all the script-writers, directors, actors and producers of our own life stories. We are all writing, directing, acting and producing a movie in which we are participating and which we are simultaneously observing. Each and every one of us is constantly projecting our perceptions onto the blank screen of life. Life is neutral: *we are the ones who choose to effect change in our lives – to make it what we wish it to be.*

Let go and soar above your life to get a bigger picture of the patterns and prejudices you are playing out again and again. Become aware of these patterns, and use them to gain clarity and perspective about what you are constantly seeking. Identify and name what is keeping you enslaved.

Recognising and remembering that we were born free and are free is something we all soon seem to forget. It is the mind that imprisons the soul – its constant chattering that drums out the soul's whisper.

Push the pause button…

Still your mind and listen carefully – this is when you will find what your soul yearns for. It is here that you will find your soul's voice. It may come as a feeling or a vision or a sound.

Wait to hear it. Allow it and encourage it to speak. Remember that the soul's voice is often quiet because of how much it has been told and trained to be silent. All the years of what Mom and Dad told us, what society told us, what life (as we know it) has told us, have possibly led us to a truth that was not ours to live.

Perhaps you have lived the way you have up to now because of what your parents, society and life "expected" you to become and do. Perhaps you thought that when you got that "title", you would feel much happier about yourself and your life; that you would be praised more and recognised as "better than the rest" by your family, friends and peers. This sense of accomplishment and harmony does not lie in the title on our business cards or in being promoted in the workplace. It lies within each and every one of us: it is a natural birthright that we all possess. We already have it!

As much as most of us have become addicted to searching outside of ourselves for happiness and contentment, in our heart of hearts we know that this search is fruitless… Because each and every one of us is the Master of our own Universe.

We were all born with a blessed gift – the gift of the Creator. We are a magnificent species that can create and shape our environment through our complex thought-process and awareness beyond what we see with our physical eyes. On the day you were born, you were given the power to create anything you wish in your life: the astounding power to manifest anything you desire. *As you imagine and speak it, so it is.*

There is, however, one thing dividing those with real power from those without. A single word describes this prerequisite that grants you the power of the Creator. This word is *"belief"*. Believe and you will see – not the other way around.

Develop the awareness, the consciousness and humble acceptance that you are the creator of your world. Be aware of the thoughts that occupy your mind and the words that come from your lips. Recognise the thoughts and words that are being projected towards you from outside yourself. Think it and it is. Speak it and it will become. The power you possess operates 24/7 as it weaves the tapestry of your existence… *Be aware.*

This power allows you to be, do and create anything you want to. This beautiful birthright places the limitless power of possibility at your fingertips… *if you believe.* So believe without a shadow of a doubt that you do possess the power of the Creator. As you believe it, so it will become – and your life will change forever. Change your thought-processes and belief systems, and you will change your world.

Now that I've reminded you about all of this, how do you feel? Is your first reaction: "Yes, I've heard all of this before" or is it resonating inside of you? *Is it ringing true?*

Do you want to journey further, deeper, higher and live a fuller life in harmony with the Universe? To be like a child – carefree and loving, full of joy and wonder? If we have wonder, we believe in the possibility of miracles: we have the hope of dreams coming true; we trust in our invisible connection to Spirit. All of these are the gifts of awakening – *awakening a life of harmony.*

I want to invite you to engage the characteristics of change: freedom, excitement, adventure, curiosity, resourcefulness, magnetism and charisma. Push against the status quo. Stop accepting things as they are and **create the space to rediscover what is right for you as an individual.** Create the space to rediscover your humanity. What feels right? What is your gut telling you? You are not a machine. You are not a hamster on a wheel. You are not a money gadget.

You are a human being with a soul. Allow yourself to feel and be human – to love, to be nurtured, to be vulnerable. It's time to silence the external voices. Stop all their screeching, demands and expectations, and listen to the soul whisper beneath all this noise saying to you: *"Let go. You are free. Let go. Being you is enough."* Recognise and acknowledge yourself for who you are. Your worth is innate. As an individual, you are a gift to this world. Celebrate this! Be your own pilot and fly on the wings of your soul – letting your soul guide you toward your bliss. Celebrate who you are! You are beautiful. You are unlimited... Celebrate your life!

Embrace your harmonious relationship with the Divine. Take a moment to feel this sacred relationship you have. This connection is yours to explore and celebrate. You are the master. You are the chosen one. Embrace your genius. Awaken harmony in your life...

Check in with yourself: does it feel like I'm going with the flow or against it? Am I flowing in harmony with myself? Do I feel in harmony with who I am? Am I in flow with my environment and those around me or do I feel like I'm constantly swimming upstream, moving against the current? Do I feel disconnected? How am I going to change to facilitate harmony in my life?

Write down your answers and pay attention to what has just been revealed from within you. All the answers you need are inside of you.

PRACTICES IN AWAKENING HARMONY

If you want to explore how to awaken harmony in your life then read on for practices aligned to assist you in doing this.

Probably the most important thing you can use to enhance the quality of how you live is the power of routine. When you repeat an exercise or new habit 28 times, it becomes a part of you. This is because the amount of energy invested decreases dramatically allowing you to complete the routine without thinking about it. You allow it to become part of you thereby creating newer, better patterns that collectively enhance your life. One of the routines I would recommend you develop to enhance your process of awakening is that of meditation.

The only way to let the spirit within you speak is to still your mind. The only way to still your mind is through meditation. Meditation holds the key to accessing the power within you. Being able to still your mind is the first step towards becoming more conscious of who you are and awakening your harmony.

In this chapter you will combine your meditation with your visualisation.

Meditation and visualisation 03: awaken HARMONY

Find a quiet space where you won't be disturbed.

Sit upright in a chair with your back supported or in the lotus position with your spine straight and your hands on your knees. Take three deep breaths. With each exhalation, feel your body and mind relax from the top of your head to the tips of your toes. When you feel completely relaxed begin your visualisation.

Feeling the Universal Energy flow through you, connect to your wisdom. Ask it to help you to awaken harmony in your life and to allow your body to naturally rebalance itself. Remember that your body knows how to do this all by itself – you just need to let go and trust it. Allow it time and space to do this. Feel yourself start to flow in balance and harmony with your loved ones, friends, family, colleagues and the entire natural world. After feeling this sense of balance and harmony for a while (10 – 15 minutes should suffice), use your breath as a guide to gently bring yourself out of meditation. Say silently to yourself: "Wide awake. I am wide awake."

Know that this visualisation will expand you, grow you and intentionally connect you with your Divine Source. You will feel completely balanced and restored to your natural radiant self. Spend some time reflecting on the wisdom and knowing that resides in your body. Honour this infinite intelligence at work.

Done once a day first thing in the morning, this visualisation will activate your positive power as a being of love.

Exercise 03: awaken HARMONY – forget fear

There is one emotion that constantly blocks our natural flow of energy. This emotion is fear. Use this exercise to rid yourself of the unnecessary fear that's blocking your path. You may need to do this a couple of times to take the process deeper.

Write down your worst fears on a piece of paper. Describe them in as much detail as you can. Keep the piece of paper in a safe place where no-one else will be able to read it. Keep it for three days. Each day re-read your list and add anything you might have left out. At the end of the third day, burn the piece of paper. As you watch it burn, feel the fear leave your being. Consciously release it. Let go of the fears that have been blocking you for too long! Bid them farewell. They have no place in your life now. Banish your fears and shine!

Affirmation 03: affirming HARMONY

Create your own set of unique affirmations that will assist you. Start with the words "I am..." Always affirm using positive language – never negative language. When you read, recite or chant your affirmation, feel it in your heart. Get in touch with what you are telling yourself. Keep it authentic. Believe it.

Some examples of affirmation to assist in awakening your HARMONY are:

I FLOW
I AM IN HARMONY
I AM IN FLOW WITH ALL AROUND ME
I AM AT EASE
I AM RELIEVED
I AM OPEN TO POSSIBILITY

Remember that your feelings activate the power within the affirmation you have created. Your feelings bring the magic into the affirmation. Always say your affirmations with love and joy.

AWAKEN CONCENTRATION "I desire"

WHERE YOUR CONCENTRATION GOES, YOUR ENERGY FLOWS.

You get what you concentrate on. If you are negative, you draw-in and experience negativity. If you are loving, you draw-in and experience love. You attract those qualities that you hold in thought and feeling because you are vibrating at the same frequency as them.

Remember: like attracts like. If you want a greater sense of peace and harmony in your life, you must embody peace and harmony. If you want to fill your life with joy then you must embody the vibration of joy. Align your concentration – thoughts, feelings and actions – with the best version of yourself you can imagine.

As I think and feel, so it is

Whenever I really want to concentrate on a task, I hear the words of my father echoing in my mind from when I was younger: "Focus Adam." My dad taught me the absolute power of concentration – he always immerses himself in whatever he does, giving his complete attention to the task at hand. Concentrate your mind and feelings on **what you do want in your life.** The more energy you spend concentrating on what you do want, the quicker you will manifest it!

Even though there will be distractions and you will be tested along the way, remain focused on what matters most to your heart. Concentrate on how you wish to feel; how you wish to love. This is an invaluable tool to navigate your path toward your highest purpose. *Remember that if this feeling makes you feel great, you are in the right place.*

Stop waiting for your life to begin. Begin to create and craft your adventure. There will be obstacles. Others will have their opinions and make judgements. Many people will have a say about how you are going about your journey. This can be positive or negative feedback – it all depends on how you internalise it. The key is to remain true to yourself. Use only that which builds and motivates you, and leave all the rest behind. Concentrate on looking deep within, allowing your inner compass to guide you. Live the dream that is you! No-one else can live it for you...

If you feel like you're stuck in a rut ask yourself: "Can I live a simpler life?" When I say "simpler", I don't mean "less than" or a life where you "lack". I am rather talking about your ability to let go of the tight grip you have on the unnecessary things in your life: the things that drain your energy; that make you feel tired just thinking about them.

I'm talking about the things that you thought you needed, but now realise you don't need any more. Concentrate on surrounding yourself with the right stuff for you, (you know what this is). This is completely possible. Think of it as an extension of you – it is who you are. Your time is now. Expanding your consciousness is key to ending your suffering. Your pain is not you. It is merely the residue of past experiences. Your pain is experienced as part of your conditioning. The second you realise this, you will liberate yourself from identifying with the pain you feel and transcend to the real you which is eternal.

Concentrate your mind and focus your heart. Connect to your joy and start living a life full of nurturing and love. Celebrate every precious moment starting right now. Remember that this moment is all that is real. Honour and bless each moment that you have been given. Expressing your individuality is your birthright. Concentrate on accessing the spark that connects you to each experience. Know that this creative energy is within you already. Focus on igniting your life and allowing this Divine Spark to surge through you until you light up like the sun! Feel alive!

Embrace your power of concentration. Take a moment to feel this infinite power right at your fingertips. This power is yours to explore and celebrate. You are the master. You are the chosen one. Embrace your genius. Awaken your concentration...

Check in with yourself: what am I concentrating on? Are they problems or solutions; obstacles or goals? Is it real success or the fear of success?

Write down your answers and pay attention to what has just been revealed from within you. All the answers you need are inside of you.

PRACTICES IN AWAKENING CONCENTRATION

If you want to explore how to awaken concentration in your life then read on for practices aligned to assist you in doing this.

Probably the most important thing you can use to enhance the quality of how you live is the power of routine. When you repeat an exercise or new habit 28 times it becomes a part of you. This is because the amount of energy invested decreases dramatically allowing you to complete the routine without thinking about it. You allow it to become part of you thereby creating newer, better patterns that collectively enhance your life. One of the routines I would recommend you develop to enhance your process of awakening is that of meditation. The only way to let the spirit within you speak is to still your mind. The only way to still your mind is through meditation. Meditation holds the key to accessing the power within you. Being able to still your mind is the first step towards becoming more conscious of who you are and awakening your power of concentration.

Meditation 04: awaken CONCENTRATION

Find a quiet space where you won't be disturbed.

Sit with your spine upright and breathe consciously. Take three deep breaths. Breathe in deeply. Hold each breath a while and then let it out through slightly pursed lips. Each time you breathe out, feel your body and mind relax completely. After completing this breathing cycle, observe your breath. Become aware of where your breath goes.

If you are struggling to concentrate, count your inhalations and exhalations. Keep your mind focused on your breath. Allow your breath to become all that is. Consciously enter a state of meditation through your breath. When you are ready (10 – 15 minutes should suffice), gently bring yourself out of meditation. Say silently to yourself, "Wide awake. I am wide awake."

This meditation is best done first thing in the morning or last thing at night. By training your mind to concentrate in this way, you will increase your power to consciously manifest that which you wish for in your life.

Visualisation 04: awaken CONCENTRATION through prayer

Prayer and intention are so important for our wellbeing. After having done your meditation in the morning, try to pray or set an intention for the day ahead before you step into it. Feel gratitude for the day you have been given. Open your heart to this gift and give thanks. Visualise the day ahead full of magic and awakening. Ignite your imagination with your feelings. Know that today is for you!

Exercise 04: awaken CONCENTRATION through practice

It is said that water is the light of the Universe made physical. Based on this, the next time you drink a glass of water, try to drink it with consciousness. Ask it to cleanse and heal your body, mind and spirit.

The power of water is often highly under-estimated. Because our bodies are made up of such a high percentage of water, they are highly receptive to our intention and the energy that we put into them through the water we drink. Toast your newfound health and energy!

Affirmation 04: affirming CONCENTRATION

Create your own set of unique affirmations that will assist you. Start with the words "I am..." Always affirm using positive language – never negative language. When you read, recite or chant your affirmation, feel it in your heart. Get in touch with what you are telling yourself. Keep it authentic. Believe it.

Some examples to assist in awakening your CONCENTRATION are:

I DESIRE
I AM LIVING CONSCIOUSLY
I AM ABLE TO CONCENTRATE MY MIND
I AM FOCUSED
I AM SUCCESSFUL
I ACKNOWLEDGE MY CREATIVE POWER

Remember that your feelings activate the power within the affirmation you have created. Your feelings bring the magic into the affirmation. Always say your affirmations with love and joy.

BE YOURSELF

Open your heart
To who you are

Acknowledge your innate value
Take in life to the full

Free your mind
So your soul can soar

Today is all you have
Love who you are today

Let go of tomorrow
To be here now

- ADAM BOTHA

AWAKEN FORGIVENESS "I love"

FORGIVING OPENS US UP TO THE FLOW OF LOVE IN OUR LIVES.

Forgiveness is one of the most incredible forces. It is the most under-rated action of love and power. It alleviates tension in the mind and body caused by the stress of holding on to anger or guilt. Permitting unforgivingness in the body poisons us and eventually makes us ill. Allowing ourselves to forgive liberates us enabling us to step toward our full potential. This makes forgiveness an essential prerequisite for growth and happiness. It activates harmony and the loving flow of energy into our lives. It opens up our channels to connection – awakening new possibilities.

I am forgiven

Forgive others. Forgive yourself. To forgive is to release the heart's burden – to free the soul from turmoil; to free the self from hatred, resentment and anger.

Hatred, resentment and anger exhaust the body's vitality and compromise the immune system. These negative emotions erode the soul's light and create unhappiness in our lives, blocking us from experiencing our higher potential. Releasing these emotions allows us to see the world around us in a positive light so that we are able to welcome the flow of abundance into our lives with open arms.

Now close your eyes and think of someone against whom you hold a grudge. Feel the grudge. Know in your heart that it is not serving you: it is harming you and the person involved. Set the intention to release this grudge. Consciously let go of it. Now try to focus a loving energy around that individual. You don't have to forgive the deed that upset you in the first place, but you do need to forgive the person. You also need to forgive yourself for holding this grudge. Feel the burden lift and notice how much lighter you feel – how much more space there is in your heart.

Imagine a world where everyone forgave everyone else. How would it feel if we all forgave ourselves for painful words spoken or harmful actions committed? Awakening forgiveness creates an awareness of light. This brings us closer to who we really are and illuminates our true nature: love.

Love is our truth, and our realisation of this truth can be more acutely felt when we forgive.

The process of awakening forgiveness is a healing art. It helps you to let go of your personal history and appreciate each and every one of your experiences. Remember that you have specifically chosen your experiences to teach you various lessons. Thank them for helping you to understand yourself better, and learn about yourself and your life and how much better it can be.

Loneliness, a lack of love, or something in you that you were told not to do could be stopping you from stepping into your dream. You might need to forgive something that prevented you from living your fantasy without guilt, naturally free from stigma and taboo. Whatever it is (your parents' aloofness, your partner's lack of attention or love you could feel, your own permission to live the way you wanted to live, your dream to really be who you were and feel supported), let it go and forgive. Just do it. Do it for you. Awakening forgiveness will give you the freedom to be who you are. Give yourself permission to forgive. Start to explore the whole of yourself – the whole of your life. Be "the way" you seek. Stop looking outside yourself. Look within. Let go of the anger and fear of yesterday, and create your own tomorrow. Lead yourself to where you need to be.

Realise that you already know where you need to be. Now go...

Embrace your power of forgiveness. Take a moment to feel this infinite power right at your fingertips. This power is yours to explore and celebrate. You are the master. You are the chosen one. Embrace your genius. Awaken your forgiveness...

Check in with yourself: who do I need to forgive? What do I need to forgive myself for? Am I in love with what I see around me? Do I love myself as I am?

Write down your answers and pay attention to what has just been revealed from within you. All the answers you need are inside of you.

PRACTICES IN AWAKENING FORGIVENESS

If you want to explore how to awaken forgiveness in your life then read on for practices aligned to assist you in doing this.

Probably the most important thing you can use to enhance the quality of how you live is the power of routine. When you repeat an exercise or new habit 28 times, it becomes a part of you. This is because the amount of energy invested decreases dramatically allowing you to complete the routine without thinking about it. You allow it to become part of you thereby creating newer, better

*patterns that collectively enhance your life. One of the routines
I would recommend you develop to enhance your process of
awakening is that of meditation.*

*The only way to let the spirit within you speak is to still your mind.
The only way to still your mind is through meditation. Meditation
holds the key to accessing the power within you. Being able to still
your mind is the first step towards becoming more conscious of who
you are and awakening your forgiveness.*

*For the purposes of this chapter you will combine your meditation
with your visualisation.*

Meditation and visualisation 05: awaken FORGIVENESS

Find a quiet space where you won't be disturbed.

Sit upright in a chair with your back supported or in the lotus position
with your spine straight and your hands on your knees. Take three deep
breaths. With each exhalation, feel your body and mind relax from the top
of your head to the tips of your toes. When you feel completely relaxed
begin your visualisation.

Visualise all those who send you negativity or those whom you still have
not forgiven. Allow yourself to feel your lack of forgiveness. Give it the time
it needs, and then hold the intention of softening this feeling. Allow it to
soften and, with all the love and forgiveness you can muster, send these
individuals radiant rose-coloured light emanating from your heart centre.
If you feel that you haven't been forgiven, say to yourself: "I am forgiven".
If you feel you need to seek forgiveness from someone, say to them in
your mind, "I am sorry. Please forgive me." You should feel a shift in your
energy immediately.

Once you feel ready (10 – 15 minutes should suffice), gently bring yourself out of meditation. Say silently to yourself: "Wide awake. I am wide awake." This meditation is best done first thing in the morning, or last thing at night. By expanding your forgiveness in this way, you will cause your auric field to expand. Too often we keep our energy contracted and small due to negative emotions that we hold onto which block the flow of love back into our lives. This meditation will allow you to let go and rejuvenate yourself by expanding your forgiveness.

Exercise 05: awaken FORGIVENESS through purification

This practice will reconnect you with positive life-giving energy by dispelling any negative residual energy clinging onto your auric field.

Salt absorbs negative energy. Try taking a "salt" or "flower" bath to cleanse and purify your auric field from any negative energy. Adding 250g of coarse sea salt to your warm bath once a week will do the trick. Alternately, collect some herbs, grasses and flowers from your garden and steep them in warm water before putting them in your bath. (To ensure that your skin won't become irritated, rub a small piece of the plant on the inside of your wrist to check).

Let go of any unforgivingness or other negative emotions you might be holding onto as you bathe. Ten to 15 minutes is all you need. Once you are done, pull the plug and allow the water to drain out with you still in the bath. Rather than drying yourself off with a towel, drip dry to allow the residue of the salt or flowers to remain on your skin. Do not use soap.

Notice how refreshed you feel afterwards. Enjoy the benefits.

Affirmation 05: affirming FORGIVENESS

Create your own set of unique affirmations that will assist you. Start with the words "I am..." Always affirm using positive language – never negative language. When you read, recite or chant your affirmation, feel it in your heart. Get in touch with what you are telling yourself. Keep it authentic. Believe it.

A great affirmation to assist your process of forgiving is: I forgive myself for holding any grudges, resentment, anger, bitterness or jealousy towards anyone in my life.

Some other examples to assist in awakening your FORGIVENESS are:

I LOVE
I FORGIVE
I AM FORGIVEN
I AM NURTURED
I NURTURE

Remember that your feelings activate the power within the affirmation you have created. Your feelings bring the magic into the affirmation. Always say your affirmations with love and joy.

AWAKEN RESPONSIBILITY *"I choose"*

ACCEPT RESPONSIBILITY FOR YOUR LIFE AS IT IS AND START
CREATING YOUR FUTURE.

Every thought, feeling and action you create has an effect. Like a drop
in the ocean of possibility, the ripples you send out always come back
to you – returning your energy to you. Become conscious and start
taking responsibility for your thoughts, feelings and actions.

Today is your gift

You are responsible for your thoughts, your words and your actions today.
They are the tools with which you "will" your creation into being. Your will be
done here on earth as it is in heaven… Heaven and earth are more intimately
connected than we think. Heaven can be here on earth (it was in the beginning)
until we started going against natural laws and upsetting the great balance of
things.

Part of this has to do with taking responsibility – being and acting responsibly.
You have the ability to magnetise yourself – pulling the things you most desire
in your life towards you. This must be done consciously and with awareness.

How do you do this? By thinking, feeling, speaking and acting your dream
into being. It is the natural process of creation: a thought becomes a feeling
which becomes a word which becomes an action that gives rise to a situation
or a thing. You therefore need to think, feel, speak and act wisely and in
accordance with the highest version of yourself. Remember that the what will
come about as a result of the how. Become your dream – resonate at the
same vibration of what it is you wish to attract through the process of creation.

Like attracts like. Be aware of what you are wishing for and inviting into your life. Know your intentions and use these responsibly.

Think back to when you were a child. Everything was a game – an adventure. Anything was an unquestioned possibility. If you wanted to experience something you could and would find a way to create it. You could imagine it! And, by imagining it, it became as real as real could be! Remember the joy and potential of everything – how you wanted the best for yourself and everybody. Compare this to your life as an adult where you're expected to conform and adapt to the norm. Most of us find ourselves constantly quizzed and questioned about whether our dreams are possible instead of being encouraged to trust what we know we want and move towards realising our full potential.

We are living in a society that is plagued by fear, doubt and oppression – that has stopped creating responsibly. You are not part of this system. Stop questioning if your dream is possible and start imagining your highest ideal. If you want it, it is there for you to experience – no matter how great or grand it might be! This is why you are here: to create your own experience!

Awakening responsibility is about being true to your essence. It's about loving what you do, and doing what you love. Find your click. Discover your groove. And then allow yourself to be who you are and do what you're here to do! Have courage. Be brave. Live your dream today.

Remember that now is all that matters, so pay careful attention to the experience you're having right now. Choose it and create it responsibly. Really live. Live now with all that you have inside of yourself. Know that you deserve an abundant life. Take a step sideways onto the path that is yours – that you have created – and start walking. Walk into your own original dream that no-one else can understand or feel except you! In walking your own true path consider that the minute we think we know ourselves completely

or that we have experienced it all, we stop the flow of abundance into
our lives. This is when the Universe shows us the flipside – "lack" – which
becomes a painful experience.

Always remain aware and grateful. There are always so many delicious
gifts to experience. We have been blessed with an abundance of endless
possibilities. Never lose your sense of responsibility as you discover these.

*Embrace yourself with reverence. Realise and love who you really
are today.*

*We are connected to a Universe that celebrates life. Today is not
just another day. It is the day that has been given to you. It holds an
infinite number of new experiences to be had. It is a gift that you will
never ever again receive in the same form, so cherish it!*

Don't allow yourself to take this day for granted. You are fooling yourself if you
do. Today is the only day of its kind and it is here for you. Acknowledge it. Be
grateful for it, and bask in the wonder and vastness of the world that has been
created for you to share.

Once we realise that this is our world and that we are here to experience
the highest version of ourselves in it, we will become lighter and vibrate at a
higher level. Know that you have the resources within to handle any situation.
You can become aware of beautiful opportunities to express yourself
authentically if you meet each day with the wonder and excitement that is
required.

It is your responsibility to be "awake".
By being awake you will create awakening in others.
By being awake you will embrace your true destiny.

By being awake you will find your life's purpose.
By being awake you will truly live.

It is time to awaken: today is your gift.

Embrace the responsibility you have for your life. Take a moment
to feel this infinite power right at your fingertips. This power is
yours to explore and celebrate. You are the master of your life. You
have chosen your own unique path. Embrace this. Awaken your
responsibility...

Check in with yourself: before you act, ask yourself about your
intention. What is my intention? How do my actions affect me?
How do my actions affect others and my environment?

Write down your answers and pay attention to what has just been
revealed within you. All the answers you need are inside of you.

PRACTICES IN AWAKENING RESPONSIBILITY

*If you want to explore how to awaken responsibility in your life then
read on for practices aligned to assist you in doing this.*

Probably the most important thing you can use to enhance the quality
of how you live is the power of routine. When you repeat an exercise
or new habit 28 times, it becomes a part of you. This is because the
amount of energy invested decreases dramatically allowing you to

complete the routine without thinking about it. You allow it to become part of you thereby creating newer, better patterns that collectively enhance your life. One of the routines I would recommend you develop to enhance your process of awakening is that of meditation.

The only way to let the spirit within you speak is to still your mind. The only way to still your mind is through meditation. Meditation holds the key to accessing the power within you. Being able to still your mind is the first step towards becoming more conscious of who you are and awakening your responsibility.

Please note that in this chapter you will combine your meditation with your visualisation.

Meditation and visualisation 06: awaken RESPONSIBILITY

Thought is a creative energy that will automatically attract whatever you are thinking. It is the seed of the creative process that brings all things into existence around you. It is up to you to create responsibly.

Sit upright in a chair with your back supported or in the lotus position with your spine straight and your hands on your knees. Take three deep breaths. With each exhalation feel your body and mind relax from the top of your head to the tips of your toes. When you feel completely relaxed begin your visualisation.

Become conscious of what you wish for in your new life: a life you are living at your highest potential. See your self as this new person who is living out their most magnificent dreams. Feel your energy as you know what you have just achieved exists as the greatest responsibility you have towards yourself. The path you have just carved for yourself is beyond your wildest dreams. You are a Divine manifestor.

Once you feel ready (10 – 15 minutes should suffice), gently bring yourself out of meditation. Say silently to yourself: "Wide awake. I am wide awake."

By awakening your responsibility in this way, you will become aware of your power as a responsible creative being. Too often we act without thinking of the effect our actions will have on our environment and those around us. This meditation will aid you to consciously expand love and wellbeing in your life. You are responsible for creating a life lived at your highest potential.

This visualisation is best done first thing in the morning or last thing at night.

Exercise 06: awaken RESPONSIBILITY for your health

Fresh fruit and vegetable juices are super-rich in antioxidants and enzymes. They will aid your digestion and boost your energy levels keeping your auric field strong and resilient.

Give juicing a try. Get yourself a juicer and start your day with fresh pineapple and carrot or grapefruit juice. End your day with a dark, leafy green juice like spinach, beetroot and carrot.

Go ahead, juice it up and feel the difference.

Affirmation 06: affirming RESPONSIBILITY

Create your own set of unique affirmations that will assist you. Start with the words "I am..." Always affirm using positive language – never negative language. When you read, recite or chant your affirmation, feel it in your heart. Get in touch with what you are telling yourself. Keep it authentic. Believe it.

Some examples to assist in awakening your RESPONSIBILITY are:

I CHOOSE
I AM RESPONSIBLE
I AM RESPONSIBLE FOR MY PATH
I CONSCIOUSLY RESPOND TO MY ENVIRONMENT
I AM IN TOUCH WITH WHO I AM
I AM WHO I AM
I BLESS THE WHOLE OF MY BEING IN THE NAME OF THE ONE
WHO IS INSIDE OF ME. AS I WILL, SO BE IT

Remember that your feelings activate the power within the affirmation you have created. Your feelings bring the magic into the affirmation. Always say your affirmations with love and joy.

HERO

Super sensory
Multi-dimensional being

Fantastic powers
Of perception

That is you
It is true

YOU are your hero
Not another

Take yourself higher
Than you thought you could go

See the bigger picture
With refreshed perspective

Share your hero
Before you leave

- ADAM BOTHA

AWAKEN GRATITUDE "I feel"

BEING GRATEFUL FOR ALL THAT WE HAVE CONNECTS US
DIRECTLY TO BEING ALIVE.

Try to remain humble and become truly grateful for what you do have,
right here and now. The Universe appreciates being appreciated. It will
reward your gratitude. Awaken gratitude in your life and use it to uplift
others and yourself. Say "thank you" more often.

Give of yourself: your time, your self, your attention. The more you give,
the more you will receive. The more you assist others, the more you will
help yourself. Allow the power of this Awakening to work in your day-to-
day life. Start to cultivate a spirit of contentment.

Thank you

What would your life be like without gratitude? If you didn't appreciate your life
and who you are? If you didn't stop to acknowledge your many gifts?

Gratitude is creative. It is the moment in time between manifestation and
realisation: that pause between creation and appreciation of what you have
just created. This magical instant is overlooked far too often.

Stop and awaken gratitude in your life. Celebrate and give thanks to
yourself for yourself! Take the time to appreciate who you are and all that
you contribute; the difference you make. Remember and acknowledge
the small miracles: those sights, sounds, smells and tastes that connect
you to your magical essence, for they are the gems that hold so much of
your power and creativity. If we can move ourselves to find the magic within

and allow our gratitude to be like that of a child shining through our being here – keeping us engaged and in awe of every delightful moment – then we will have found our true purpose.

If you were to write a pledge to yourself to increase your sense of gratitude, what would it be? Could it sound something like this:

I pledge to be grateful for the talents I have been blessed with, to stay excited about my life and to make choices that keep me connected to my purpose. I pledge to honour my place within the matrix of creation, to accept my greatness within this creation whilst remaining humble. I pledge to be involved in my own life: to activate my life with passion, love and appreciation.

I would recommend writing your own pledge for yourself. Write it from your heart so as to activate the awakening of your new life. Use it to ignite your vision of the future.

We are living in times that demand a certain pace to the point of us becoming addicted to chaos and speed. We have forgotten to pause, reflect and be grateful for the small things: the roof over our heads, food on the table, family and friends who love and care about us, and the very unique and personal connection we have with the Universe.

I've realised my own addiction is due to lack of self love because I am afraid. Afraid of what I'm becoming: the cold, corporate, rigid, do-it-by-the-book guy.

If you are unhappy with who you are right now, you might feel the need to escape. Rather identify and confront the issue of not being happy (not being happy with yourself, not being happy with your environment that you have created) and choose to change it. Start by asking yourself a new question: "How do I transform myself and my life?"

I can choose again

What if you have been the one holding yourself back?
What if it has been you all along?

It's time for you to explore all of your options. It's time for you to release all of your fears and make positive life-changing decisions for yourself. It's time for you to be thankful for everything you have in your life.

It's time you thanked yourself for all that you have manifested in your life up until now. Cherish and hold dear in your heart all that you are. It's time for you to humble yourself and see that you have enough to be happy with right here, right now. Everything you need is provided for you. Set the intention to choose what is right for you.

Recognise that your soul's nourishment resides within you. Acknowledge this by saying thank you to the energy you came from. See and realise your inner connection to why you are here. Be grateful for this.

Take a moment to feel infinite gratitude in your heart. Feel this for everyone and everything in your life. This connection is yours to explore and celebrate. Awaken your gratitude and a spirit of contentment.

Check in with yourself: am I grateful for what I have right here and now? Express this to yourself, others and the greater consciousness. Do I feel sincere appreciation for the gifts in my life? Can I feel this in my heart? Do I appreciate who I am? Do I accept being appreciated for who I am?

Write down your answers and pay attention to what has just been revealed within you. All the answers you need are inside of you.

PRACTICES IN AWAKENING GRATITUDE

If you want to explore how to awaken gratitude in your life then read on for practices aligned to assist you in doing this.

Probably the most important thing you can use to enhance the quality of how you live is the power of routine. When you repeat an exercise or new habit 28 times, it becomes a part of you. This is because the amount of energy invested decreases dramatically allowing you to complete the routine without thinking about it. You allow it to become part of you thereby creating newer, better patterns that collectively enhance your life. One of the routines I would recommend you develop to enhance your process of awakening is that of meditation.

The only way to let the spirit within you speak is to still your mind. The only way to still your mind is through meditation. Meditation holds the key to accessing the power within you. Being able to still your mind is the first step towards becoming more conscious of who you are and awakening your gratitude.

Please note that in this chapter you will combine your meditation with your visualisation.

Meditation and visualisation 07: awaken GRATITUDE

Find a quiet space where you won't be disturbed.

Sit upright in a chair with your back supported or in the lotus position with your spine straight and your hands on your knees. Take three deep breaths. With each exhalation feel your body and mind relax from the top of your head to the tips of your toes. When you feel completely relaxed begin your visualisation.

Introduce the intention of gratitude. Start with the small things in life: be grateful for the food on your plate, the sun on your skin and the breeze on your face. Now extend your gratitude to include the roof over your head, your family and friends, your daily adventures and the abundance in your life.

Focus on each and celebrate them one by one.

Now move your attention to your heart centre and imagine a radiant pink light shining within you. Feel love and gratitude radiating from your heart centre out into the world. Continue to expand this light and feeling until the entire planet is surrounded, radiating a beautiful pink glow. Once you feel ready (10 –15 minutes should suffice), gently bring yourself out of meditation. Say silently to yourself: "Wide awake. I am wide awake."

This meditation is best done first thing in the morning or last thing at night.

Your intention of love and gratitude will increase the vibrational energy of love and gratitude in your life and all around you. By holding this intention you are increasing the collective consciousness of love and gratitude on the planet.

Exercise 07: awaken GRATITUDE through feeling

Spend 10 minutes a day getting in touch with your feelings. Sit undisturbed and take three deep breaths, focusing on your heart centre where you process all your feeling. Remain aware of how you are feeling without judgement or thinking. Let your feelings flow through you without getting attached to them. Feel, process, observe and release them.

Extend the 10 minute intervals as you feel more comfortable. Remember that your power and your truth lie in your feelings. Be grateful for the truth of who you are.

Affirmation 07: affirming GRATITUDE

Create your own set of unique affirmations that will assist you. Start with the words "I am..." Always affirm using positive language – never negative language. When you read, recite or chant your affirmation, feel it in your heart. Get in touch with what you are telling yourself. Keep it authentic. Believe it.

Some examples to assist in awakening your GRATITUDE are:

I AM GRATEFUL
I AM LOVE
I AM ABUNDANT
I AM BLESSED
I AM A BLESSING

Remember that your feelings activate the power within the affirmation you have created. Your feelings bring the magic into the affirmation. Always say your affirmations with love and joy.

AWAKEN SURRENDER "I trust"

SURRENDER TO YOUR HIGHEST POTENTIAL.

Surrender yourself to the change that you really want in your life. Then, as strange as this may sound to you (because we have always been told to control everything in case something goes wrong), detach from the outcome and trust in the Universal intelligence that's at work for you. Get out of your own way and see how all external obstacles remove themselves. Enjoy all of the enriching aspects of your life. Allow any negativity to flow through you without resistance and without holding onto it.

Take only that which will benefit you and grow you! Surrender to the ultimate bliss taking shape in your life.

Allow yourself to be-come

Giving yourself permission to become all you wish yourself to be is the greatest gift you can give yourself. Step into the dream that is yours. Surrender to the path of your highest potential and start walking.

Your time is now. You are meant to feel unending life every moment from here on. You deserve to be living your life completely "awake". You are worthy of all encompassing fulfilment. You are enough as you are. Give yourself permission to shine as brightly as you can! Know that you are all you need to be.

Part of surrendering to your authentic life is moving on if you find yourself in a place or situation that does not serve your highest purpose or make you feel more alive. When you connect with your "aliveness" you become who you are meant to be. Yes, you will have to walk through the obstacles and shadows to get there, but this is all part of the work you need to do to "awaken".

Your shadows are the parts of yourself that you are not conscious of yet They often control you through old fears and patterns that dominate much of your behaviour. Once you become aware of your shadows, you will begin living consciously and create the freedom to choose how you wish to live your life – and who you wish to be.

Allowing yourself to become involves feeling your shadow, knowing your shadow, embracing your shadow. Having embraced it, look it straight in the eye. Connect with it and say, "Shadow, I acknowledge and embrace you. I appreciate the strength you have given me. It's time for you to step out of my way. Move aside now to allow Universal light to illuminate my life." Surrender to the abundance in your life. Relinquish your hold on the material things that weigh you down and begin trusting the wealth of riches within you: riches that you just need to be open to receiving. Receive these with grace and give them with joy. Understand this great circle of life – that being in a state of grace brings about an inner joy. This is all yours once you just allow it to be! Surrender to the light you are meant to share with yourself and others.

Believe that you are so much more than you think you are: you are a being who has been blessed with a unique personal connection to all your fellow sentient beings

You are the custodian of your fellow brothers and sisters.

It is up to you to protect and take care of them. Take this opportunity to acknowledge your role within the world. You are part of this great symphony of life. You have been given unique power to conduct a very sacred part of this symphony of creation. It is up to you to accept, embrace and activate this role in your life. Open your heart and let the sweet music of your life in.

Awakening surrender involves trusting yourself and your soul's purpose.
It involves recognising that you are "the one" you've been searching for your
whole life. You are supported by a powerful and dynamic team of guides,
guardians and angels in the spiritual realm. They are around you, watching your
every move to make sure you're okay. They are there to guide you and they love
you. Their purpose is to serve and protect you throughout your experiences on
this planet. They are calling your name right now and trying to get you to listen to
their message, and awaken to a life richer in love and purpose.
"Wake up loved one to what's going on around you. Look and really see it for
yourself. Take a long hard look at what you see. Then decide: decide to either
carry on living the way you've been living or choose again."

Do you feel yourself in a void of materialism, of disconnection with Mother Nature
and all those you love and are a part of you? It's time for you to take the reigns
tightly in your hands and make a positive impact on the world around you.
Decide to make a difference. It really is up to you!

Every time I hear someone say, "I'll do it tomorrow", I fear for the heart of this
person who takes it for granted that tomorrow is guaranteed to them (as if
they're under the illusion that they're in control of being given tomorrow).

Do it now. Decide to make a difference and take action now. We have so little
time here as it is, so choose to impact positively on this beautiful planet we live
on. We are the custodians of this miracle of Mother Earth. Her soul is intimately
connected to ours. Can't we feel her pain? Can't we hear her crying out to all
of us: "Save me from destruction. Save me and save yourselves."

We can never "own" Mother Earth because she will never belong to us.
Right now she needs our help though. She needs the help of those who,
once again, are beginning to feel their connection to her (like the invisible,

powerful, loving, lifelong connection between a mother and child).

This awesome responsibility and blessing has been placed squarely in our hands. Let's embrace it with love and the utmost care in our hearts. Let's all step outside of the prison of consumerism and into the light of living consciously, ensuring sustainability for all humankind and Mother Earth.

Release yourself

To release is to create.

The law of the Universe is such that when we let go of something that we have so desperately wanted and imagined in our lives – bam! It manifests! If we cling onto what we wish for (which we have been taught to do our entire lives), and desire to create out of fear of lack or emptiness, we stop the flow of Divine energy through us. We block our creative energy instead of just allowing it to be and surrendering to it.

In awakening surrender, we start to challenge our programming and conditioning. Consider that we have been taught to resist the flow of Divine energy our entire lives! We have bought into a system that by and of its nature keeps us prisoner and serving it as our master (its primary objective).

How does it do this? By convincing us that we don't have enough because we are not enough. In this way, it's constantly selling us things we don't need – promising us a sense of fulfilment and bliss through the purchase of a car, clothes, a mobile phone… It keeps shoving the "next best deal" down our throat, guaranteeing instant happiness. Happiness? How can something outside of ourselves buy us happiness? Especially when the happiness we are talking about is not the momentary thrill of a new something or other but rather lasting, fulfiling, true happiness that is guaranteed to last a lifetime!

Take the time to ask yourself which energy you serve. One grounded in materialism or one that feeds your soul? One of momentary thrill or one that takes you to a place where you naturally feel you belong? What is this belief system that we have been buying into for so long? Why have we allowed ourselves to be captivated and consumed by it? At some or other level I'm sure you will feel this truth resonating in your gut. Know that no matter how much money and material "stuff" you surround yourself with in order to feel safe and secure, you will carry on feeling afraid that you don't have enough and that you aren't enough unless you consciously change this pattern.

Surrender to your life and soul's purpose. Awaken to the truth that you are enough as you are right now. You have all that can bring you ultimate bliss. It's there inside you! It has been there all along – you just haven't been listening. Hear your soul's voice. Feel it calling you to the abundance available to you. Release yourself from the distractions of the world.

Still your mind and listen carefully to what your soul is yearning for. It knows what you are really seeking: greater joy and fulfilment. Find your purpose and bliss. In surrendering to your purpose, realise that you were born with natural gifts and abilities – abilities unique to you that you may have forgotten, that made you feel good about yourself and what you could bring to the world. They came to you naturally and with ease when you were younger. They will do so again. You just need to allow them. Your soul will help you to rediscover them if you just listen to it.

But, here's a word of caution: once you decide to listen to your soul, you cannot stop listening. So be sure about your choice to step onto this path toward your bliss, because once you tap into your calling as a human being on this planet, it's all you will care about. Nothing else will matter because you will be doing and feeling so fulfilled. You will surrender to your purpose every single day of your life, and discover the real reason why you are here.

Just let go, breathe and trust… Everything will manifest perfectly. And, with the Universe holding the bigger picture, everything will manifest at exactly the right time too! In perfect balance and harmony. Remember that the Universe knows exactly what you want and is working in accordance with all that is to bring you exactly what you wish for.

Trust the process and keep watching your thoughts.
Take a moment to feel infinite gratitude in your heart. Feel this for everyone and everything in your life. This connection is yours to explore and celebrate. Awaken your surrender.

Check in with yourself: have I done all that I possibly can to realise my soul's desire? Have I let go of the outcome by surrendering it to a source of energy greater than myself? Do I trust the higher power that is taking care of me? Or am I holding onto my negative patterns or to people that no longer serve my wellbeing? Am I holding myself back or am I allowing ultimate bliss to take shape in my life?

Write down your answers and pay attention to what has just been revealed from within you. All the answers you need are inside of you.

PRACTICES IN AWAKENING SURRENDER

If you want to explore how to awaken surrender in your life then read on for practices aligned to assist you in doing this.
Probably the most important thing you can use to enhance the quality of how you live is the power of routine. When you repeat an exercise

or new habit 28 times, it becomes a part of you. This is because the amount of energy invested decreases dramatically allowing you to complete the routine without thinking about it. You allow it to become part of you thereby creating newer, better patterns that collectively enhance your life. One of the routines I would recommend you develop to enhance your process of awakening is that of meditation.
The only way to let the spirit within you speak is to still your mind.
The only way to still your mind is through meditation. Meditation holds the key to accessing the power within you. Being able to still your mind is the first step towards becoming more conscious of who you are and awakening your ability to surrender.

In this chapter you will combine your meditation with your visualisation.

Meditation and visualisation 08: awaken SURRENDER

Find a quiet space where you won't be disturbed.

Sit with your spine upright and breathe consciously. Take three deep breaths. Breathe in deeply, hold each breath a while and then let it out through slightly pursed lips. Each time you breathe out, feel your body and mind relax completely.

When you are completely relaxed imagine yourself as water flowing down a mountain. Take time to surrender to the feeling. Swirl, eddy and flow. Bubble and pool – gently and then more rapidly. How do you feel? Concentrate on the details. Immerse yourself in this feeling. Start flowing faster and faster until you tumble over a waterfall.

Be present on this journey. Let go. Give into the feeling of what it truly feels like to surrender. Surge and run until you arrive at the ocean. Stream into the big blue. What does it feel like to become part of this vastness, this magnificence?

Spend as much time as you need to here. When you are ready, slowly become aware of the sounds in the room. Feel the blood flowing into your hands and feet, and say silently to yourself, "Wide awake. I am wide awake."

Exercise 08: awaken SURRENDER through laughter

In our stress-filled lives, we have forgotten what it feels like to really laugh from our core...

Laughter raises our vibration. It releases endorphins (chemicals that make us feel good) into our brains. It creates a flow of positive energy and is a beautiful form of surrender.

Spend five minutes a day laughing. It doesn't matter whether you watch a comedy or a funny movie, have a great conversation with a friend, spend time with children, think of a funny memory or even just sit and pull faces at yourself in front of the mirror. Laugh until your stomach aches. Really let go and allow yourself to be consumed by your joy.

Affirmation 08: affirming SURRENDER

Create your own set of unique affirmations that will assist you. Start with the words "I am..." Always affirm using positive language – never negative language. When you read, recite or chant your affirmation feel it in your heart. Get in touch with what you are telling yourself. Keep it authentic. Believe it.

Some examples to assist in awakening your SURRENDER are:

I TRUST
I LET GO

I SURRENDER
I ALLOW MYSELF TO FLOW THROUGH LIFE
I AM ALLOWING MY LIFE
I ALLOW _____ TO FLOW INTO MY LIFE

Remember that your feelings activate the power within the affirmation you have created. Your feelings bring the magic into the affirmation. Always say your affirmations with love and joy.

ABUNDANCE

Relinquish your tight grip
On the material things you hold
That hold you so tightly

Trust there to be enough for us all
Abundance is yours

Accept with grace
Release with joy
Knowing the great circle of life

All is yours once you accept it!

\- ADAM BOTHA

AWAKEN PURPOSE "I belong"

YOU ARE HERE FOR A REASON.

Your life is not a set of random events that happen by chance. You have a specific role to play on this earth, and it is up to you to take the time and energy to discover what it is and create it. You are a crucial part of the whole. You bring with you an exquisitely original energy to the world. It is now up to you to explore, discover and live your life's purpose.

You will know you have found your life's purpose by how "alive you feel" when doing it. You will feel the change that you are making in your heart – creating infinite happiness within yourself. Thank yourself for being you.

Human (race) to human (kind)

When you woke up today, how did you feel? Did you say to yourself, "Get up! Get up or you're going to be late!" If you had to say this to yourself then perhaps you're not doing what makes you truly happy; you aren't naturally excited about what you're doing with your life.

Too many of us make a living as opposed to making a life. We fool ourselves into thinking that our job is what makes us happy but, deep down inside, we know that we are not living our purpose and it feels almost too painful to face.

Awakening your purpose requires you to take a long hard look at your life, and ask yourself what is preventing you from doing what it is you love: what it is you're here to do. Very often, deep seated emotional pain lies beneath what we feel creating certain patterns of behaviour. In many cases, this comes from our childhood – being teased at school for example or feeling abandoned by our parents or loved ones. These feelings need to be engaged and healed in order to move on and lead a life of purpose.

Despite this, the pattern of behaviour that most of us play out is to try and cover up this pain. Instead of confronting it and feeling it, we spend our hard-earned money on things we don't really need in an attempt to make ourselves feel better. The tragedy lies in the fact that unless we feel, accept and understand our shadow side, we will unconsciously carry on playing out this behaviour and further delay our healing.

Rather than cover up what you really feel with more and more things, ask yourself the question: "Where is my authentic self in all of this? Is it already operational in my life or is it hiding somewhere underneath the deep-seated emotions within me that I am unwilling to feel?"

By not feeling, facing or accepting our emotions, we deny the shadow parts of ourselves that have been suppressed for so long. To change this pattern of suppression and awaken to our soul's purpose, we have to overcome our fear of feeling anger, hate and hurt – feelings that threaten to consume and destroy us. By suppressing and denying this fear, we are subconsciously giving it power and control over our lives. By pretending it isn't there and refusing to acknowledge it, we give it unbelievable power over our lives – and in our lives. And, until we decide to own it, it will own us.

The only way to move into the light is to shine consciousness into the shadow... Into your shadow. Your shadow self is made up of all of your negative destructive traits or habits that keep playing themselves out, often without you even being conscious of them. To own your shadow, you firstly need to become aware of this side of you.

One of the best ways to start identifying your shadows is to look at any negative results that have manifested in your life – anything that is "unwanted".

Once you know what these are, dig a little deeper and ask why these things are in your life and why you attracted them. Ask your authentic self what lesson you need to learn from these negative experiences. You can only release your unwanted patterns once you are conscious of them. Sitting down and writing honestly about yourself helps uncover the obstacles that the shadow puts in the way to prevent you from realising your highest purpose.

The moment you become aware of the control the shadow side has had over you and why this was necessary, you can free yourself.

Remember that the shadow and the light have co-existed from the dawn of time. Both shape and create the full experience of our lives, and we would not understand the one without the other. Embrace the fact that you are a whole being who has come to this earth to experience the whole of who you are – and have the courage to step into this and discover and live your purpose.

Rather than allowing any suppressed emotions to control your life, take back your power by becoming more conscious. Start to acknowledge and understand the whole of "who you are". Recognise your wholeness and begin to live without being afraid of experiencing or becoming more than you could ever imagine.

Be yourself

Nowhere in this vast expanse of forever will there ever be anyone like you or with your specific purpose. You are a unique, special individual who occupies this time and space – here and now – sharing your gifts and making an impact.

Recognise that every other being you meet is exactly the same as you: one of a kind. This goes against how we generalise and categorise ourselves into tribes of colour, creed and age. By looking beyond these, we start to discover the truth of our miraculous wonderful selves!

The truth is that we will never again be who we are right now: that we are, by our very nature, our own registered trademark. We have been blessed with the unique copyright of our own lives – the right to be ourselves and live our purpose freely and soulfully.

You are an original, holding space in this Universe – exploring it in your own special way. Celebrate why you are here and the gifts you have to share. Embrace your purpose and make it manifest. Be yourself like no-one else!

Take a moment to feel your purpose. Feel this for everyone and everything in your life. This connection is yours to explore and celebrate. Awaken your purpose and the passion in your life.

Check in with yourself: what makes me feel truly alive? Am I doing this as much as I can? Are my actions and way of life in line with the highest, brightest, most amazing version of myself? If not, why? What do I need to do to get back onto my path?

Write down your answers and pay attention to what has just been revealed from within you. All the answers you need are inside of you.

PRACTICES IN AWAKENING PURPOSE

If you want to explore how to awaken purpose in your life then read on for practices aligned to assist you in doing this.

Probably the most important thing you can use to enhance the quality of how you live is the power of routine. When you repeat an exercise or new habit 28 times, it becomes a part of you. This is because the amount of energy invested decreases dramatically, allowing you to complete the routine without thinking about it. You thereby create newer, better patterns that collectively enhance your life. One of the routines I would recommend you develop to enhance your process of awakening is that of meditation.

The only way to let the spirit within you speak is to still your mind. The only way to still your mind is through meditation. Meditation holds the key to accessing the power within you. Being able to still your mind is the first step towards becoming more conscious of who you are and awakening your purpose.

Meditation 09: awaken PURPOSE

Silence holds a very special magic. It puts you in touch with who you are and gives your soul space to "speak". Make time at the beginning and end of each day to sit and be silent without distraction.

Close your eyes, regulate your breathing and just sit. Listen to the silence. Allow your body, mind and spirit to recalibrate and balance themselves. Sit like this for 10 – 15 minutes. Ask the nature of your true purpose. Let go and trust. Listen carefully to what you receive and try not to judge it: this message is for you. Shhh... Listen.

Visualisation 09: awaken PURPOSE within your energy field

After completing the above meditation in the morning, stay seated and half close your eyes. Visualise a bright golden sun shining within your solar plexus. Feel it grow and expand until you are completely surrounded with golden light. Know that this golden light protects and energises you. Internalise the words "I am gold" or "in my world, I am the sun". As you sit like this, feel your worth. Acknowledge and value your worth. Know that you are safe and protected as you leave to start your day.

Exercise 09: awaken PURPOSE through journaling

Writing is an important form of self-expression and release. It can help you identify themes and patterns in your life – leading you to your life's purpose.

Buy yourself a notebook or journal and start to write each day. Even if it's just a short paragraph about how you feel or something you've been thinking about lately, make a note of your thoughts and feelings, and reflect on what's going on inside you. Get into the habit of expressing yourself using pen and paper. This will help you to stay connected to yourself and identify and release elements of your shadow self.

You can also use your writing to set your intentions and manifest these into being. To do this, write in the present as if you are already where you would like to be – and that your dream has come true. Trust that what you are expressing will be made real in one way or another. Be aware of your words: they are infinitely powerful. Be sure to be specific about what it is that you want and why. Also be clear about the Universe's role in assisting you to live your purpose.

Affirmation 09: affirming PURPOSE

Create your own set of unique affirmations that will assist you. Start with the words "I am..." Always affirm using positive language – never negative language. When you read, recite or chant your affirmation, feel it in your heart. Get in touch with what you are telling yourself. Keep it authentic. Believe it.

Some examples to assist in awakening your PURPOSE are:

I BELONG
I ALLOW MY TRUE PURPOSE TO MAKE ITSELF KNOWN TO ME
I AM LIVING MY TRUE PURPOSE
I AM ALIGNED WITH MY HIGHEST POTENTIAL
I CAN BE WHO AND WHAT I WILL TO BE
I AM WHO I WISH MYSELF TO BE
I AM ENOUGH

Remember that your feelings activate the power within the affirmation you have created. Your feelings bring the magic into the affirmation. Always say your affirmations with love and joy.

DARE TO SAY

I am who I am
Because I chose to be me
I am where I am because
I am choosing my journey

I am free and unbound
I am in love with the life
That I am creating
This is my adventure
This is my journey

Dare to say

I feel incredible gratitude for being
A blessed witness to this Creation
That excites and invigorates me

Dare to say

This is my journey
and I'm loving it!

- ADAM BOTHA

THE BEGINNING
THE WAY FORWARD

All of who you are and who you are becoming is in your hands. You have the world at your fingertips. THE LIFE YOU ARE CREATING IS REALLY UP TO YOU.

Now that you understand and have familiarised yourself with practising the Nine Awakenings, you have created a pathway for your transformation – changing how you think and feel, and aligning your energy field in order to be more open and charged with life-giving energy and purpose.

You have awakened and will never be the same again...

By expanding your awareness and acknowledging your connection to all that is, you will find yourself in harmonic resonance with the Universe. Understand that you have power over your mind because of your ability to concentrate on what you are creating. Open your heart to forgiving and take responsibility for your life. Be grateful and give thanks for being alive. Let go, surrender and live "in flow" with your essence.

Awaken to your true purpose of living your highest potential. Feel alive now. Realise that you are the Universe's miracle.

Believe this. Know this. And become this. May your life be blessed and abundant throughout every moment.

Love,
Adam.

Adam Botha: soul-space creator; spiritual explorer; new consciousness catalyst; metaphysical guide; transformational storyteller, design lecturer and book cover designer.

Adam lives in the quiet suburb of Melville in Johannesburg, South Africa. He has immersed himself in metaphysical and meta-vibrational energy work for the last 15 years. Working as a creative director, his journey has led him to discover magic and purpose beyond the illusion of who he thought he was – and could or should be. Today he uses his design skills and creativity as a tool for his transformational work, sharing this with others through his workshops, blogs, interactions and now this book.

Adam believes that every single human being has the right to discover and live their highest potential: "Do what you love, for it is the legacy you will leave behind one day when all you take with you are your experiences."

Adam has attended the following courses and experiential workshops:

Abundance Awareness
(course in metaphysics and energy work)
– Derek Welensky

Tai Chi Chuan retreat
(experiential martial arts retreat)
– Sifu Leo Ming

The Inner Lovers Workshop
(self-discovery and transformation)
– Miriam Rawicz and Adele Gruber

The Enneagram Workshop
(transpersonal psychology: profiling the nine personality types)
– Pam Roux

Coaching Essentials
(meta-coaching and NLP introduction certified by the *International Society of Neuro-Semantics*)
– Cheryl Lucas and Carey Jooste

Ayahuasca Ceremony
(two day ceremony hosted by Peruvian shaman)
– Golbert Grandez, Carlos and Elizma

Recovery Coaching Training Programme
– David Collins, Lila Lieberman and Amanda Gilford

The Transformational Author's Writing Experience (transformational author seminar)
– Christine Kloser

Ongoing personal life coaching with Isabel Vidal (modelled on the work originated by Caroline Myss), and self-realisation work with Antony Tarboton.